The Ultimate Confectionery Cookbook

Dishes, Volume 11

Olivia Bennett

Published by B&H Publishing Group, 2025.

While every precaution has been taken in the preparation of this book, the publisher assumes no responsibility for errors or omissions, or for damages resulting from the use of the information contained herein.

THE ULTIMATE CONFECTIONERY COOKBOOK

First edition. February 24, 2025.

Copyright © 2025 Olivia Bennett.

ISBN: 979-8230373490

Written by Olivia Bennett.

Table of Contents

To the dreamers who find joy in a swirl of caramel, the artists who sculpt sweetness from sugar, and the bakers whose kitchens glow with the warmth of homemade treats.

To my family and friends, who have always been my sweetest inspiration and the first to taste every creation—your love and encouragement mean everything.

And to all who believe that life is better with a little more sugar—this book is for you. Keep creating, keep sharing, and keep savoring every moment.

Introduction to Confectionery: A World of Sweet Possibilities

Confectionery, the art of making sweet treats, is a craft that has delighted people for centuries. From the humble beginnings of honey-based sweets to the intricate creations of modern pastry chefs, confectionery embodies creativity, precision, and a universal love for sweetness. This chapter explores the history and cultural significance of confectionery, provides an overview of essential ingredients and tools, and offers tips for both beginners and seasoned professionals to embark on or refine their candy-making journey.

A Brief History of Confectionery

1. Ancient Origins

The roots of confectionery can be traced back thousands of years, long before the advent of refined sugar:

- Honey as Nature's Sweetener: Ancient Egyptians used honey to create simple confections, often combining it with nuts and fruits.

- Candied Fruits and Nuts: In ancient Greece and Rome, people preserved fruits and nuts in honey, creating an early form of candy.

2. The Introduction of Sugar

The discovery and refinement of sugar revolutionized confectionery:

- Medieval Europe: Sugar was initially a luxury item used for medicinal purposes and elaborate desserts in royal courts.

- The Islamic Golden Age: Confectioners in the Middle East pioneered techniques like candying and sugar pulling, influencing global practices.

3. The Industrial Revolution

The 18th and 19th centuries saw advancements in confectionery:

- Mass Production: Innovations in sugar refinement and machinery enabled the large-scale production of sweets like toffee and hard candies.

- Chocolate: The invention of the cocoa press in the 19th century made chocolate more accessible, leading to iconic confections.

4. Modern Day

Today, confectionery blends tradition with innovation:

- Artisanal Revival: Small-scale confectioners emphasize high-quality ingredients and craftsmanship.

- Technological Advancements: Modern tools like tempering machines and silicone molds make intricate designs more accessible.

Cultural Significance of Confectionery

Confectionery plays a vital role in cultural traditions and celebrations around the world:

- Festivals and Holidays: From candy canes at Christmas to Turkish delight during Eid, sweets are integral to festive occasions.

- Symbolism: In many cultures, sweets symbolize joy, prosperity, and love, often given as gifts or shared during milestones.

- Regional Specialties: Every region has its unique confections, from French nougat to Japanese mochi, showcasing local ingredients and techniques.

Overview of Ingredients, Tools, and Techniques

1. Essential Ingredients

Understanding the core ingredients is crucial for success in confectionery:
- Sugar:
- Types: Granulated, brown, powdered, and specialty sugars like turbinado.
- Role: Provides sweetness, structure, and caramelization.
- Sweeteners:
- Alternatives: Honey, maple syrup, agave nectar, and corn syrup.
- Usage: Prevents crystallization and adds unique flavors.
- Dairy:

- Ingredients: Milk, cream, butter, and condensed milk.
- Role: Adds richness and helps create smooth textures in fudge and caramels.
- Chocolate:
- Varieties: Dark, milk, white, and couverture.
- Techniques: Tempering for shine and snap, melting for molding and coating.
- Fruits and Nuts:
- Uses: Adds flavor, texture, and decoration.
- Popular Choices: Almonds, hazelnuts, dried fruits, and citrus zest.
- Stabilizers and Gelling Agents:
- Ingredients: Gelatin, pectin, agar-agar, and egg whites.
- Role: Creates structure in gummies, marshmallows, and nougat.

2. Essential Tools

Equipping yourself with the right tools makes confectionery both easier and more precise:
- Thermometers:
- Candy thermometers are essential for monitoring sugar stages (soft ball, hard crack, etc.).
- Cookware:
- Heavy-bottomed saucepans ensure even heat distribution.
- Molds:
- Silicone molds for shapes, chocolate molds for pralines, and lollipop molds for hard candies.
- Mixing Tools:
- Sturdy spatulas, whisks, and stand mixers for blending and aeration.
- Cutting Tools:
- Sharp knives for brittle, and cookie cutters for shaping.
- Decorating Equipment:
- Piping bags, edible glitter, and food-safe brushes for artistic touches.

3. Techniques for Success

Mastering these techniques lays the foundation for advanced confectionery:

- Cooking Sugar:
- Control heat carefully to avoid burning or crystallization.
- Use a clean, damp pastry brush to wash down sugar crystals from the pan's sides.
- Tempering Chocolate:
- Melt chocolate gently, then cool and reheat to specific temperatures for a glossy finish.
- Gelatin Blooming:
- Soak gelatin in cold water before use to ensure smooth incorporation.
- Flavor Layering:
- Balance sweetness with complementary flavors like salt, spices, or citrus.
- Decoration:
- Practice piping and drizzling techniques to enhance visual appeal.

Tips for Beginners and Professionals

1. For Beginners

- Start Simple:
- Begin with basic recipes like fudge, hard candies, or chocolate bark.
- Invest in Quality Tools:
- A good candy thermometer and sturdy saucepan are non-negotiable.
- Be Patient:
- Precision and timing are key. Rushing through steps can lead to mistakes.
- Understand Sugar Stages:
- Familiarize yourself with terms like soft ball, firm ball, and hard crack.

2. For Professionals

- Refine Techniques:
- Experiment with advanced methods like sugar pulling, isomalt casting, or chocolate airbrushing.
- Focus on Ingredients:
- Source premium-quality chocolate, nuts, and flavorings for superior results.
- Innovate with Flavors:

- Infuse ganaches with teas, spices, or spirits to create unique confections.
- Develop Signature Styles:
- Incorporate your artistic flair through custom molds, colors, or designs.

Common Challenges and Solutions

1. Crystallization
   - Problem: Sugar crystals forming during cooking.
   - Solution: Add an acid like lemon juice or corn syrup to stabilize the mixture.
   2. Overheating
   - Problem: Burnt caramel or scorched chocolate.
   - Solution: Use moderate heat and monitor closely with a thermometer.
   3. Uneven Texture
   - Problem: Grainy fudge or brittle caramel.
   - Solution: Stir consistently and follow precise timing.

The Joy of Confectionery

Confectionery is more than just creating sweets—it's about crafting joy, indulging the senses, and connecting with others. Whether you're a novice exploring the basics or a seasoned professional pushing boundaries, the journey through confectionery is as rewarding as the final product. This book will guide you step-by-step, from understanding foundational techniques to mastering advanced creations, ensuring you have the tools and knowledge to create delectable treats for every occasion.

Prepare your tools, gather your ingredients, and embark on this delightful adventure into the world of confectionery. Let's make magic, one sweet treat at a time.

Chapter 1: The Science of Sugar

Sugar is the cornerstone of confectionery, acting as the primary ingredient in countless sweet creations. Understanding the science behind sugar is essential for crafting candies, syrups, and other confections with the desired texture and flavor. This chapter delves into the stages of sugar cooking, explores the tools needed for precise temperature control, and provides foundational recipes such as Simple Syrup, Caramel Syrup, and Hard Candy Base.

The Chemistry of Sugar

At its core, sugar is a carbohydrate that plays multiple roles in cooking and baking. In confectionery, sugar is transformed through heat and manipulation, creating everything from soft caramels to brittle toffee.

1. The Composition of Sugar

- Types of Sugar:
    - Sucrose: The most common form, derived from sugarcane or sugar beets.
    - Fructose and Glucose: Found in fruits and honey, often used as additives to prevent crystallization.
    - Solubility:
    - Sugar dissolves in water, creating solutions of varying concentrations. These solutions change properties as they are heated, a process crucial to candy-making.

Stages of Sugar Cooking

Cooking sugar transforms its structure, creating different textures and flavors. Each stage corresponds to a specific temperature range, determined by the amount of water evaporated during cooking.
    1. Thread Stage (230–234°F / 110–112°C)
    - Appearance: Thin threads form when a small amount of syrup is dropped into cold water.
    - Uses: Simple syrups, glazing fruits, and light sugar coatings.

2. Soft Ball Stage (235–240°F / 113–116°C)

- Appearance: Syrup forms a soft, pliable ball in cold water.

- Uses: Fudge, pralines, and fondant.

3. Firm Ball Stage (245–250°F / 118–121°C)

- Appearance: Syrup forms a firm ball that retains its shape but is still malleable.

- Uses: Caramels, nougat, and marshmallows.

4. Hard Ball Stage (250–266°F / 121–130°C)

- Appearance: Syrup forms a hard ball that is pliable when pressed.

- Uses: Divinity, rock candy, and some toffees.

5. Soft Crack Stage (270–290°F / 132–143°C)

- Appearance: Syrup forms strands that bend before breaking.

- Uses: Taffy and butterscotch.

6. Hard Crack Stage (295–310°F / 146–154°C)

- Appearance: Syrup forms brittle strands that break easily.

- Uses: Hard candies, lollipops, and brittle.

7. Caramel Stage (320–350°F / 160–177°C)

- Appearance: Sugar melts completely, turning amber as it caramelizes.

- Uses: Caramel sauce, toffee, and spun sugar.

Tools for Accurate Temperature Control

Precision is vital in sugar cooking. Even slight temperature deviations can drastically alter the final product.

1. Candy Thermometers

- Why Use Them:

- Accurate readings are essential for achieving specific sugar stages.

- Types:

- Analog: Durable and reliable for high temperatures.

- Digital: Provides quick, precise readings with user-friendly displays.

2. Infrared Thermometers

- Non-contact thermometers that measure surface temperature. Ideal for situations where traditional thermometers are impractical.

3. Ice Water Test

- A traditional method to determine sugar stages without a thermometer:
    1. Drop a small amount of syrup into a bowl of cold water.
    2. Observe the texture and consistency to identify the stage (e.g., soft ball, hard crack).

4. Essential Tools for Heat Management

- Heavy-Bottomed Saucepans: Even heat distribution prevents hotspots and burning.
    - Pastry Brush: Dip in water to wash down sugar crystals on the pan's sides.
    - Heat-Resistant Spatula: Ensures thorough stirring without melting.

Basic Recipes

1. Simple Syrup

Simple syrup is a versatile ingredient used in beverages, glazing, and baking.
    Ingredients:
    - 1 cup granulated sugar
    - 1 cup water
    Instructions:
    1. Combine sugar and water in a saucepan.
    2. Heat over medium heat, stirring until the sugar dissolves.
    3. Bring to a boil, then remove from heat. Cool before using.
    Uses:
    - Sweetening cocktails, moistening cakes, and glazing fruit.

2. Caramel Syrup

Caramel syrup adds depth and complexity to desserts and beverages.
    Ingredients:

- 1 cup granulated sugar
- 1/4 cup water
- 1/2 cup heavy cream
- 2 tablespoons butter
- Pinch of salt

Instructions:

1. Combine sugar and water in a saucepan over medium heat.

2. Stir until sugar dissolves, then stop stirring. Let the mixture boil until it turns amber.

3. Remove from heat and carefully whisk in cream and butter. Stir in salt.

4. Cool before transferring to a jar.

Uses:

- Drizzling over ice cream, flavoring lattes, and enhancing baked goods.

3. Hard Candy Base

This recipe forms the foundation for lollipops, candy canes, and more.

Ingredients:

- 2 cups granulated sugar
- 2/3 cup water
- 2/3 cup light corn syrup
- Flavoring and coloring (optional)

Instructions:

1. Combine sugar, water, and corn syrup in a saucepan. Stir to combine.

2. Heat over medium heat without stirring until the mixture reaches 300°F (hard crack stage).

3. Remove from heat and add flavoring and coloring. Stir gently.

4. Pour onto a silicone mat or into molds. Let cool completely before removing.

Uses:

- Crafting lollipops, candy shapes, and brittle.

Common Challenges in Sugar Cooking

Even experienced confectioners encounter challenges when working with sugar. Here's how to address some common issues:

1. Crystallization
   - Cause: Undissolved sugar crystals re-form during cooking.
   - Solution: Add an acid (e.g., lemon juice) or an invert sugar (e.g., corn syrup) to stabilize the mixture.
   2. Burning
   - Cause: High heat or insufficient stirring.
   - Solution: Use medium heat and monitor closely with a thermometer.
   3. Sticky Candies
   - Cause: Insufficient cooking or humidity during cooling.
   - Solution: Cook to the correct temperature and store in airtight containers.

The Art and Science of Sugar

Mastering the science of sugar transforms your confectionery skills, opening the door to endless possibilities. From the simplest syrup to intricate caramel creations, sugar cooking is a foundational skill that combines precision, patience, and creativity. Armed with knowledge of sugar stages, the right tools, and these basic recipes, you're ready to embark on a journey into the sweet world of confectionery. Each step will build your confidence and expertise, allowing you to craft confections that delight and inspire. Let the magic of sugar guide your creativity and elevate your sweets to new heights.

Chapter 2: Chocolate Creations

Chocolate is one of the most beloved ingredients in the world of confectionery. Its rich flavor, velvety texture, and versatility make it a staple for countless recipes and techniques. Whether tempering chocolate for glossy finishes, molding it into stunning shapes, or dipping fruit and candies, mastering chocolate is a rewarding journey. This chapter will guide you through essential chocolate techniques like tempering, molding, and dipping, provide recipes for Chocolate Truffles, Chocolate Bark, and Chocolate-Covered Strawberries, and address common challenges such as blooming and seizing.

Understanding Chocolate

1. The Composition of Chocolate

Chocolate is made from cocoa beans and consists of three key components:
- Cocoa Solids: Contribute to chocolate's flavor and color.
- Cocoa Butter: Provides a smooth texture and enables tempering.
- Sugar and Milk: Added for sweetness and creaminess in milk and white chocolate.

2. Types of Chocolate

- Dark Chocolate: Contains at least 50-70% cocoa solids. Rich and intense, ideal for tempering and truffles.
- Milk Chocolate: Includes milk solids, making it sweeter and creamier.
- White Chocolate: Contains no cocoa solids, only cocoa butter, sugar, and milk, offering a mild, sweet flavor.

3. Choosing High-Quality Chocolate

For the best results:
- Opt for chocolate with a high percentage of cocoa butter (couverture chocolate).
- Avoid chocolate chips, as they contain stabilizers that prevent smooth melting.

Working with Chocolate

Mastering chocolate requires understanding its behavior, especially when heating and cooling. These techniques are fundamental to creating professional-quality chocolate confections.

1. Tempering Chocolate

Tempering is the process of heating, cooling, and reheating chocolate to align its cocoa butter crystals. Proper tempering results in a glossy finish, firm texture, and a satisfying snap.

- Why Temper Chocolate?
- Prevents blooming (discoloration caused by fat or sugar crystals).
- Creates a stable structure for molding and dipping.
- Methods of Tempering:
- Seeding Method:

1. Melt two-thirds of the chocolate over a double boiler or in the microwave, heating to 113–122°F (45–50°C) for dark chocolate or 104–113°F (40–45°C) for milk/white chocolate.

2. Remove from heat and stir in finely chopped chocolate (the "seed") until the temperature drops to 84–86°F (29–30°C).

3. Gently reheat to 88–90°F (31–32°C) for dark chocolate or 86–88°F (30–31°C) for milk/white chocolate.

4. Test by spreading a small amount on parchment. If it hardens with a glossy finish, it's tempered.

- Tabling Method:

1. Melt chocolate as above.

2. Pour two-thirds onto a marble slab and work it with a spatula until it cools to the desired temperature.

3. Return it to the bowl, mixing to combine and bring it to temper.

2. Molding Chocolate

Molding is the process of pouring tempered chocolate into molds to create shapes.

- Steps:

1. Ensure molds are clean and dry.

2. Pour tempered chocolate into the mold, tapping to release air bubbles.

3. Scrape off excess chocolate with a bench scraper.

4. Let set at room temperature or refrigerate briefly for easy release.

- Uses: Chocolate bars, pralines, and decorative shapes.

3. Dipping Chocolate

Dipping involves coating items like fruits, nuts, or candies in tempered chocolate.

- Steps:

1. Use a fork or dipping tool to submerge the item in tempered chocolate.

2. Lift and let excess chocolate drip off.

3. Place on parchment to set.

- Tips:

- Work quickly to prevent chocolate from cooling.

- Sprinkle toppings (nuts, sea salt) immediately before the chocolate sets.

Recipes

1. Chocolate Truffles

Chocolate truffles are a luxurious confection, combining creamy ganache centers with a rich chocolate coating.

Ingredients:

- 8 oz (225 g) dark chocolate, finely chopped

- 1/2 cup heavy cream

- 1 tablespoon unsalted butter

- Optional: Flavorings like liqueurs, extracts, or spices

- Cocoa powder, chopped nuts, or tempered chocolate for coating

Instructions:

1. Heat cream and butter in a saucepan until just simmering.

2. Pour over chopped chocolate and let sit for 2 minutes. Stir until smooth.

3. Add flavorings if desired. Cover and refrigerate for 1–2 hours, or until firm.

4. Scoop teaspoon-sized portions, roll into balls, and coat with cocoa powder, nuts, or tempered chocolate.

5. Store in an airtight container in a cool place.

2. Chocolate Bark

Chocolate bark is a simple yet elegant treat that allows endless customization with toppings.

Ingredients:

- 12 oz (340 g) tempered dark, milk, or white chocolate

- Toppings: Nuts, dried fruits, crushed candies, or sea salt

Instructions:

1. Line a baking sheet with parchment paper.

2. Pour tempered chocolate onto the parchment and spread evenly.

3. Sprinkle toppings evenly over the chocolate.

4. Let set at room temperature or refrigerate until firm.

5. Break into pieces and store in an airtight container.

3. Chocolate-Covered Strawberries

A classic dessert, chocolate-covered strawberries are easy to make and perfect for special occasions.

Ingredients:

- 1 lb (450 g) fresh strawberries, washed and dried thoroughly

- 8 oz (225 g) tempered dark, milk, or white chocolate

Instructions:

1. Hold each strawberry by the stem and dip into tempered chocolate, coating evenly.

2. Let excess chocolate drip off before placing on parchment paper.

3. Optional: Drizzle with contrasting chocolate or sprinkle with nuts.

4. Let set at room temperature or refrigerate briefly.

Troubleshooting Common Chocolate Problems

Working with chocolate can be challenging, but understanding common issues helps ensure success.

1. Blooming

- Cause: Improper tempering or storage conditions.
    - Types:
    - Fat Bloom: Greasy streaks caused by unstable cocoa butter crystals.
    - Sugar Bloom: White patches caused by moisture dissolving sugar on the surface.
    - Solution:
    - Temper chocolate correctly.
    - Store in a cool, dry place away from humidity.

2. Seizing

- Cause: Chocolate coming into contact with water, causing it to clump.
    - Solution:
    - Gradually add a small amount of warm cream or butter to restore smoothness.
    - Avoid introducing moisture by keeping tools and bowls completely dry.

3. Overheating

- Cause: Excessive heat breaking down cocoa butter and causing graininess.
    - Solution:
    - Melt chocolate gently using a double boiler or short bursts in the microwave.
    - Monitor temperature with a thermometer.

Advanced Techniques for Chocolate Creations

Once comfortable with basic techniques, you can explore advanced chocolate artistry:
    - Airbrushing: Use an edible airbrush to spray color or cocoa butter designs onto molds.
    - Texturing: Use textured mats or stencils to create patterns on chocolate.
    - Layering: Create multi-layered bars with contrasting flavors and textures.

Conclusion

Mastering the art of chocolate opens up endless possibilities for creating stunning confections. Techniques like tempering, molding, and dipping lay the foundation for a range of recipes, from indulgent truffles to eye-catching chocolate bark and elegant chocolate-covered strawberries. By understanding common challenges and how to overcome them, you can confidently craft professional-quality treats. Whether you're making gifts, party favors, or personal indulgences, chocolate creations will always bring a touch of sweetness and sophistication to your culinary repertoire. Let this chapter inspire you to explore, experiment, and embrace the delicious world of chocolate artistry.

Chapter 3: Fudge and Creamy Candies

Fudge and creamy candies hold a special place in the world of confectionery, offering rich, velvety textures and indulgent flavors. Perfect for gifting, celebrations, or personal enjoyment, these treats are both versatile and satisfying to make. Achieving the perfect consistency in fudge requires an understanding of the delicate balance between ingredients, temperature, and technique. This chapter explores methods for crafting smooth, creamy fudge, provides recipes for Classic Chocolate Fudge, Peanut Butter Fudge, and Marshmallow Fudge, and offers ideas for creating variations with nuts, fruits, and flavored extracts.

The Art of Making Fudge

Fudge, a semi-soft candy with a melt-in-your-mouth texture, is made by combining sugar, butter, and milk, then heating the mixture to a specific temperature before cooling and beating it to the desired consistency. The result is a decadent treat that can be customized with various flavors and mix-ins.

1. The Science Behind Fudge

Understanding the science of fudge-making is crucial for consistent results:
   - Sugar Crystals:
   - Fudge is an emulsion of sugar crystals suspended in a fat-rich liquid. The goal is to create tiny sugar crystals for a smooth texture.
   - Temperature:
   - The sugar mixture must reach the correct temperature (soft ball stage, 235–240°F / 113–116°C) to achieve the ideal consistency.
   - Cooling and Beating:
   - Cooling the mixture undisturbed prevents premature crystallization. Beating introduces air and controls the formation of sugar crystals, resulting in a creamy texture.

2. Common Challenges in Fudge-Making

- Grainy Texture:

- Caused by large sugar crystals or premature crystallization. To avoid this, ensure sugar is fully dissolved before boiling and avoid stirring once the mixture starts to boil.

- Soft or Sticky Fudge:

- Indicates the sugar mixture didn't reach the proper temperature. Use a candy thermometer to ensure accuracy.

- Crumbly Fudge:

- Caused by overcooking or overbeating. Follow precise timing and monitor consistency.

Techniques for Smooth, Creamy Fudge

1. Preparing Ingredients

- Use high-quality ingredients, as the simplicity of fudge amplifies their flavor.

- Measure ingredients accurately, as even small deviations can affect the texture.

2. Cooking the Mixture

- Combine sugar, butter, and milk in a heavy-bottomed saucepan to ensure even heat distribution.

- Heat gently and stir until sugar dissolves completely before increasing the temperature.

3. Monitoring Temperature

- Use a candy thermometer to track the temperature accurately.

- Cook to the soft ball stage (235–240°F / 113–116°C) for traditional fudge.

4. Cooling the Mixture

- Transfer the saucepan to a cool surface or water bath and let the mixture cool undisturbed to 110°F (43°C). This step ensures a smooth consistency when beaten.

5. Beating and Setting

- Beat the cooled mixture with a wooden spoon or electric mixer until it thickens and loses its gloss.

- Pour into a greased or parchment-lined pan and let set at room temperature.

Classic Fudge Recipes

1. Classic Chocolate Fudge

This timeless recipe creates rich, chocolatey fudge with a smooth texture.

Ingredients:

- 2 cups granulated sugar
- 3/4 cup whole milk
- 2 oz unsweetened chocolate, chopped
- 1/4 cup unsalted butter
- 1 teaspoon vanilla extract

Instructions:

1. Combine sugar, milk, chocolate, and butter in a heavy-bottomed saucepan.

2. Heat over medium heat, stirring until sugar dissolves and mixture boils.

3. Cook without stirring until the mixture reaches 235°F (soft ball stage).

4. Remove from heat and add vanilla. Do not stir.

5. Let cool to 110°F, then beat until thickened and no longer glossy.

6. Pour into a greased 8x8-inch pan and smooth the top. Let set for 2–3 hours before cutting into squares.

2. Peanut Butter Fudge

This creamy, nutty fudge is perfect for peanut butter lovers.

Ingredients:

- 2 cups granulated sugar
- 1/2 cup whole milk
- 1/2 cup unsalted butter
- 1 cup peanut butter (creamy or crunchy)
- 1 teaspoon vanilla extract

Instructions:

1. Combine sugar, milk, and butter in a saucepan. Heat over medium heat, stirring until sugar dissolves.

2. Bring to a boil and cook until the mixture reaches 235°F.

3. Remove from heat and stir in peanut butter and vanilla until smooth.

4. Pour into a greased 8x8-inch pan and let set for 2 hours. Cut into squares.

3. Marshmallow Fudge

Marshmallows add a light, airy texture to this decadent fudge.

Ingredients:

- 1 1/2 cups granulated sugar
- 1/2 cup evaporated milk
- 1/2 cup unsalted butter
- 2 cups mini marshmallows
- 1 1/2 cups semisweet chocolate chips
- 1 teaspoon vanilla extract

Instructions:

1. Combine sugar, evaporated milk, and butter in a saucepan. Heat over medium heat, stirring until mixture boils.

2. Cook for 4 minutes, stirring constantly.

3. Remove from heat and stir in marshmallows, chocolate chips, and vanilla until smooth.

4. Pour into a greased 8x8-inch pan and let set for 2 hours. Cut into squares.

Creative Variations

Fudge is endlessly customizable. Experiment with these ideas to create unique flavors:

1. Add-Ins

- Nuts: Walnuts, pecans, or almonds add crunch and balance sweetness.

- Fruits: Dried cranberries, cherries, or apricots provide tangy contrast.

2. Flavor Extracts

- Replace vanilla with almond, peppermint, or orange extract for a twist.

3. Layered Fudge

- Create visual appeal by layering two or more flavors, such as chocolate and peanut butter.

4. Themed Fudge
- Add food coloring and sprinkles for festive occasions like Christmas or Halloween.

Troubleshooting and Tips

1. Grainy Fudge
   - Ensure sugar dissolves completely before boiling.
   - Avoid stirring during cooking to prevent crystal formation.
   2. Soft or Sticky Fudge
   - Cook to the correct temperature (soft ball stage).
   - Allow fudge to set completely at room temperature before cutting.
   3. Overcooked or Crumbly Fudge
   - Use a candy thermometer for precise temperature control.
   - Stop beating once the mixture thickens and loses its gloss.

Fudge as a Gift

Fudge makes an excellent homemade gift. Use these ideas to package it attractively:
   - Boxes and Tins: Line with parchment paper and arrange fudge neatly.
   - Cellophane Bags: Tie with ribbon for an elegant presentation.
   - Custom Labels: Add handwritten notes or decorative tags with flavor descriptions.

Conclusion

Fudge and creamy candies epitomize indulgence, offering endless possibilities for flavor and presentation. With techniques for smooth, creamy textures, foundational recipes like Classic Chocolate Fudge, Peanut Butter Fudge, and Marshmallow Fudge, and creative variations, you're equipped to master this timeless confection. Whether crafting treats for yourself or sharing as gifts, fudge is a versatile and rewarding addition to your confectionery repertoire. Let this chapter inspire you to explore the art of fudge-making and create sweet memories with every bite.

Chapter 4: Caramel Confections

Caramel is a versatile and beloved confection that ranges from soft, chewy candies to crunchy, brittle toffees. Its rich, buttery flavor and golden hue make it a favorite in desserts and candies alike. Mastering caramel-making requires an understanding of the precise science behind cooking sugar, the art of balancing ingredients, and the patience to perfect texture and flavor. This chapter delves into crafting perfect caramels, provides recipes for Salted Caramel, Caramel Apples, and Toffee, and offers practical tips for avoiding crystallization and other common challenges.

The Essence of Caramel

Caramel is made by cooking sugar until it melts and undergoes a chemical process called caramelization. During this process, the sugar transforms into a complex mixture of compounds, giving caramel its distinctive flavor and color.

1. The Stages of Caramel

Caramel can be tailored to different textures and applications depending on how it is cooked:

- Soft Caramel (Chewy): Perfect for candy or fillings; cooked to 245–250°F (firm ball stage).

- Firm Caramel (Hard): Used for crunchy toffees or coatings; cooked to 300°F (hard crack stage).

- Liquid Caramel: Used in sauces or drizzles; cooked until amber and deglazed with cream or butter.

Key Ingredients in Caramel

1. Sugar

- Granulated sugar is the most common choice for caramel. Avoid brown sugar unless a specific flavor is desired, as its molasses content can affect the texture and consistency.

2. Dairy

- Cream: Adds richness and smoothness, especially in soft caramels and sauces.

- Butter: Enhances flavor and creates a glossy finish.

3. Liquid Sweeteners

- Corn Syrup: Prevents crystallization and ensures a smooth texture.

- Honey or Maple Syrup: Adds a distinct flavor but can alter the texture.

4. Flavor Enhancers

- Salt: Balances sweetness and enhances caramel's depth.

- Vanilla or Other Extracts: Adds aromatic complexity.

The Science of Caramelization

1. How Sugar Melts

As sugar is heated, it first melts into a clear liquid. The longer it cooks, the more water evaporates, and the sugar molecules break down into caramel compounds.

2. Temperature Control

Precision is crucial in caramel-making:

- Use a reliable candy thermometer to monitor the temperature accurately.

- Adjust heat levels carefully to avoid burning or uneven cooking.

3. Avoiding Crystallization

Crystallization occurs when sugar molecules bond together, forming a grainy texture. To prevent this:

- Use a damp pastry brush to wash down sugar crystals from the sides of the pan.

- Avoid stirring once the sugar starts boiling.

- Add corn syrup or an acidic ingredient (e.g., lemon juice) to inhibit crystal formation.

Crafting Perfect Caramel

1. Chewy Caramels

Chewy caramels are cooked to the firm ball stage (245–250°F). They should hold their shape but remain pliable.

2. Soft Caramel Sauce

For drizzling or dipping, cook the sugar to a lower temperature (220–230°F) and add cream or butter to achieve a pourable consistency.

3. Firm Toffee

Toffee is caramel cooked to the hard crack stage (300°F), resulting in a brittle texture perfect for candy bars or as a base for nuts and chocolate.

Recipes

1. Salted Caramel

This rich, buttery caramel with a hint of salt is perfect for candies, sauces, or toppings.

Ingredients:
- 1 cup granulated sugar
- 1/4 cup water
- 6 tablespoons unsalted butter, cubed
- 1/2 cup heavy cream
- 1 teaspoon sea salt

Instructions:

1. Combine sugar and water in a saucepan. Heat over medium heat, swirling gently to dissolve sugar.

2. Allow the mixture to boil undisturbed until it turns amber (350°F).

3. Remove from heat and carefully whisk in butter, followed by cream. Stir until smooth.

4. Add salt and let cool before using or storing.

2. Caramel Apples

Caramel-coated apples are a festive treat, perfect for parties and holidays.

Ingredients:
- 6 medium apples, washed and dried
- 1 cup granulated sugar
- 1/2 cup light corn syrup
- 1/2 cup heavy cream
- 1/4 cup unsalted butter

- 1/4 teaspoon salt
- Optional toppings: chopped nuts, sprinkles, or chocolate drizzle

Instructions:

1. Insert sticks into the tops of the apples and set aside.

2. Combine sugar, corn syrup, cream, butter, and salt in a saucepan. Heat over medium heat, stirring until sugar dissolves.

3. Cook without stirring until the mixture reaches 245°F (firm ball stage).

4. Remove from heat and let cool slightly. Dip apples into the caramel, swirling to coat evenly.

5. Add toppings if desired, then place on parchment paper to set.

3. Toffee

Toffee combines the rich flavor of caramel with a brittle texture, often topped with chocolate and nuts.

Ingredients:

- 1 cup unsalted butter
- 1 cup granulated sugar
- 1/4 cup light corn syrup
- 2 tablespoons water
- 1/2 teaspoon salt
- 1 teaspoon vanilla extract
- Optional toppings: chopped nuts or chocolate chips

Instructions:

1. Combine butter, sugar, corn syrup, water, and salt in a saucepan. Heat over medium heat, stirring until sugar dissolves.

2. Cook without stirring until the mixture reaches 300°F (hard crack stage).

3. Remove from heat and stir in vanilla.

4. Pour onto a greased baking sheet, spreading evenly.

5. Sprinkle with toppings while warm. Let cool completely before breaking into pieces.

Variations and Enhancements

1. Flavor Variations

- Spiced Caramel: Add cinnamon, nutmeg, or ginger for warmth.

- Coffee Caramel: Infuse cream with coffee before adding it to the caramel.
2. Add-Ins
- Nuts: Stir in toasted pecans, almonds, or hazelnuts for texture.
- Fruit: Fold in dried cranberries or cherries for a tangy contrast.

3. Decorative Touches

- Drizzle caramel over desserts or chocolates for a luxurious finish.
- Use caramel as a glue to adhere edible decorations like sprinkles or edible glitter.

Troubleshooting Caramel

Caramel-making can be tricky, but most issues are preventable with the right techniques:
1. Grainy Caramel
- Cause: Crystallization during cooking.
- Solution: Avoid stirring after the sugar dissolves. Use corn syrup to stabilize the mixture.
2. Burnt Caramel
- Cause: Overheating or uneven heat.
- Solution: Monitor temperature closely and use a heavy-bottomed saucepan for even heat distribution.
3. Runny Caramel
- Cause: Undercooking or insufficient cooling time.
- Solution: Ensure the caramel reaches the correct temperature and allow it to set fully.

Storage and Presentation

Proper storage ensures your caramel confections stay fresh and delicious:
- Soft Caramels: Wrap individually in wax paper and store in an airtight container at room temperature for up to two weeks.
- Toffee: Store in a tin or airtight container with parchment paper between layers to prevent sticking.

- Caramel Sauce: Keep in a sealed jar in the refrigerator for up to one month. Reheat gently before use.

Conclusion

Caramel is a confectionery staple, offering endless possibilities for texture, flavor, and creativity. Whether you're crafting chewy salted caramels, coating apples for a festive treat, or making brittle toffee, mastering the techniques of caramel-making is a rewarding skill. With the recipes and tips in this chapter, you're well-equipped to explore the rich world of caramel confections, creating treats that delight both the palate and the eye. Let the magic of caramel inspire your culinary creativity, one golden creation at a time.

Chapter 5: Hard Candies and Lollipops

Hard candies and lollipops are timeless confections that captivate with their vibrant colors, glossy finishes, and playful designs. Whether you're creating fruity lollipops, classic peppermint discs, or buttery butterscotch drops, crafting these sweets requires precision, creativity, and a touch of artistry. In this chapter, we'll explore the tools and techniques needed for making vibrant, clear hard candies, share detailed recipes, and dive into creative shapes and designs using molds.

Understanding Hard Candies

Hard candies are made by cooking sugar to a high temperature (usually the hard crack stage, around 300°F/150°C), then cooling it into solid shapes. The process involves manipulating sugar's physical properties to create a brittle, glass-like texture.

1. The Science of Hard Candies

Hard candies rely on precise temperature control:

- Sugar Stage: Cooking to the hard crack stage ensures the candy hardens properly.

- Humidity Matters: Hard candies are hygroscopic, meaning they absorb moisture from the air. Proper storage is crucial to maintain their texture.

2. Characteristics of Hard Candies

- Clear Appearance: Achieved by controlling crystallization during cooking.

- Firm and Brittle Texture: Ensures candies snap when bitten.

- Intense Flavors: Often achieved using concentrated flavoring oils or extracts.

Tools for Making Hard Candies and Lollipops

Equipping yourself with the right tools ensures success in creating professional-quality hard candies and lollipops.

1. Essential Tools

- Candy Thermometer: Accurate temperature readings are critical for reaching the hard crack stage.

- Heavy-Bottomed Saucepan: Ensures even heat distribution, reducing the risk of burning.

- Silicone Mats or Parchment Paper: Prevents sticking and makes cleanup easier.

- Heat-Resistant Spatulas: Ideal for stirring hot sugar mixtures.

2. Specialized Tools

- Molds:
    - Lollipop Molds: Designed with stick holders for creating lollipops.
    - Candy Molds: Available in various shapes for themed designs.
    - Dropper or Squeeze Bottle: Useful for precise pouring into molds.
    - Lollipop Sticks: Essential for crafting lollipops.
    - Pastry Brush: Helps wash down sugar crystals from the sides of the pan.

Techniques for Vibrant, Clear Hard Candies

1. Preparing the Sugar Mixture
    - Combine sugar, water, and corn syrup in a saucepan.
    - Stir over medium heat until the sugar dissolves completely. Avoid stirring once the mixture starts boiling to prevent crystallization.
    2. Monitoring Temperature
    - Use a candy thermometer to cook the mixture to 300°F (hard crack stage).
    - Remove from heat immediately to avoid burning.
    3. Adding Colors and Flavors
    - Use gel or liquid food coloring for vibrant hues. Add sparingly to maintain clarity.

- Incorporate concentrated flavoring oils or extracts off the heat to preserve their potency.

4. Pouring into Molds

- Work quickly to pour the hot mixture into molds or onto a silicone mat.

- For lollipops, place sticks in molds before pouring the mixture.

5. Cooling and Demolding

- Allow candies to cool completely at room temperature. Avoid refrigeration, as it can introduce moisture.

- Gently release candies from molds once they've hardened.

Recipes

1. Fruit-Flavored Lollipops

These colorful lollipops are perfect for parties, gifts, or nostalgic treats.

Ingredients:

- 2 cups granulated sugar
- 2/3 cup light corn syrup
- 2/3 cup water
- Gel food coloring (various colors)
- 1 teaspoon concentrated flavoring oil (e.g., cherry, lemon, or orange)
- Lollipop sticks

Instructions:

1. Prepare lollipop molds by greasing lightly or lining them with parchment paper. Place sticks in molds.

2. Combine sugar, corn syrup, and water in a saucepan. Heat over medium heat, stirring until sugar dissolves.

3. Stop stirring and bring the mixture to a boil. Cook to 300°F (hard crack stage).

4. Remove from heat and add food coloring and flavoring oil. Stir gently.

5. Pour the mixture into molds, ensuring sticks are fully embedded.

6. Let cool completely before removing from molds.

2. Peppermint Discs

Classic peppermint discs are refreshing, versatile, and easy to make.

Ingredients:

- 2 cups granulated sugar
- 2/3 cup light corn syrup
- 2/3 cup water
- Red gel food coloring
- 1 teaspoon peppermint oil

Instructions:

1. Line a baking sheet with a silicone mat or parchment paper.

2. Combine sugar, corn syrup, and water in a saucepan. Heat over medium heat, stirring until sugar dissolves.

3. Cook to 300°F without stirring. Remove from heat and add peppermint oil.

4. Divide the mixture into two portions. Add red food coloring to one portion and leave the other clear.

5. Pour alternating red and clear stripes onto the baking sheet, using a skewer to swirl the colors.

6. Allow to cool, then break into discs.

3. Butterscotch Drops

These golden-hued candies offer a buttery, caramel-like flavor.

Ingredients:

- 1 cup granulated sugar
- 1/2 cup light corn syrup
- 1/4 cup unsalted butter
- 1/4 cup water
- 1 teaspoon vanilla extract

Instructions:

1. Combine sugar, corn syrup, butter, and water in a saucepan. Heat over medium heat, stirring until sugar dissolves.

2. Bring to a boil and cook to 300°F (hard crack stage).

3. Remove from heat and stir in vanilla extract.

4. Drop spoonfuls of the mixture onto a silicone mat to form individual candies.

5. Let cool completely before storing.

Creative Shapes and Designs Using Molds

1. Themed Candy Molds
   - Use molds in shapes like animals, hearts, or holiday motifs to create personalized candies.
   - Grease molds lightly with a neutral oil for easy release.
2. Layered Colors
   - Create multi-colored candies by pouring layers of different colored sugar mixtures. Let each layer set slightly before adding the next.
3. Embedded Elements
   - Embed edible decorations like edible glitter, dried flowers, or sprinkles in the candy for a unique look.
4. Swirled Designs
   - Use two or more colors and swirl them together with a skewer or toothpick for a marbled effect.

Troubleshooting Common Issues

1. Cloudy or Grainy Candies
   - Cause: Crystallization during cooking.
   - Solution: Avoid stirring once the sugar mixture boils. Add corn syrup to stabilize the sugar.
2. Sticky Candies
   - Cause: High humidity or undercooking.
   - Solution: Store candies in an airtight container with desiccant packs. Cook to the correct temperature.
3. Burning
   - Cause: Overcooking or uneven heating.
   - Solution: Use a heavy-bottomed saucepan and monitor temperature closely.

Packaging and Storing Hard Candies

Proper storage ensures that your candies remain crisp and vibrant:

1. Airtight Containers

- Store candies in a cool, dry place to prevent them from absorbing moisture.

2. Individual Wrapping

- Wrap each candy in cellophane or wax paper to prevent sticking and maintain freshness.

3. Decorative Packaging

- Use jars, tins, or custom boxes for gifting. Add labels or ribbons for a festive touch.

Conclusion

Hard candies and lollipops are a delightful addition to any confectioner's repertoire. With their eye-catching colors, playful shapes, and customizable flavors, they offer endless opportunities for creativity. By mastering the techniques for vibrant, clear candies and experimenting with recipes like Fruit-Flavored Lollipops, Peppermint Discs, and Butterscotch Drops, you can craft treats that bring joy to every occasion. Let this chapter inspire you to explore the art of hard candy-making, turning simple ingredients into edible works of art.

Chapter 6: Marshmallows and Nougat

Marshmallows and nougat, with their light, airy textures and endless flavor possibilities, are quintessential confections that delight both the young and the young at heart. Whether enjoyed on their own, melted into hot cocoa, or incorporated into more elaborate treats, these confections are versatile and satisfying to make at home. This chapter explores techniques for achieving the perfect textures, shares recipes for Vanilla Marshmallows, Rocky Road Bars, and Honey Nougat, and offers ideas for creating flavored and colored variations for festive occasions.

The Basics of Marshmallows and Nougat

1. What Are Marshmallows?

Marshmallows are soft, spongy confections made by whipping a sugar syrup with gelatin. Air is incorporated into the mixture to create their characteristic fluffy texture.

2. What Is Nougat?

Nougat is a dense, chewy confection made by whipping sugar syrup into egg whites. It can range from soft and chewy to firm and brittle, depending on the recipe and cooking method.

3. Similarities and Differences

- Both marshmallows and nougat rely on aeration to achieve their textures.

- Marshmallows are gelatin-based and have a spongy consistency, while nougat uses egg whites and has a chewier, often nutty profile.

Achieving Light, Airy Textures

The key to perfect marshmallows and nougat lies in the balance of ingredients, temperature control, and proper whipping.

1. Temperature Control

- Use a candy thermometer to ensure sugar syrups reach the correct temperature.

- For marshmallows, cook syrup to the *soft ball stage* (240°F / 116°C).

- For nougat, cook syrup to the *firm ball stage* (248°F / 120°C) or higher, depending on desired firmness.

2. Whipping

- Proper aeration is essential for light textures.

- Use a stand mixer with a whisk attachment for consistent whipping.

- For marshmallows, whip until the mixture is thick but still pourable.

- For nougat, whip until the mixture forms stiff peaks.

3. Setting

- Allow marshmallows and nougat to set in molds or pans lined with parchment paper or dusted with powdered sugar to prevent sticking.

- Let them cool completely at room temperature for the best texture.

Recipes

1. Vanilla Marshmallows

Classic vanilla marshmallows are a perfect base for customization or enjoying as-is.

Ingredients:

- 3 packets unflavored gelatin (about 7.5 teaspoons)

- 1/2 cup cold water (for blooming gelatin)

- 2 cups granulated sugar

- 2/3 cup light corn syrup

- 1/2 cup water

- 1/4 teaspoon salt

- 1 teaspoon vanilla extract

- 1/2 cup powdered sugar (for dusting)

- 1/4 cup cornstarch (for dusting)

Instructions:

1. Line a 9x13-inch pan with parchment paper and dust with a mixture of powdered sugar and cornstarch.

2. Bloom gelatin by sprinkling it over 1/2 cup cold water in the bowl of a stand mixer.

3. Combine sugar, corn syrup, 1/2 cup water, and salt in a saucepan. Heat over medium heat until sugar dissolves.

4. Increase heat and cook without stirring until the mixture reaches 240°F.

5. With the mixer on low, slowly pour the hot syrup into the gelatin. Gradually increase speed and whip until thick and fluffy (about 8–10 minutes).

6. Add vanilla extract and mix briefly.

7. Pour the mixture into the prepared pan and spread evenly with a spatula. Dust the top with powdered sugar mixture.

8. Let set for 4–6 hours or overnight. Cut into squares and coat sides with powdered sugar mixture.

2. Rocky Road Bars

A rich, chocolatey treat packed with marshmallows, nuts, and a touch of crunch.

Ingredients:

- 2 cups semisweet chocolate chips
- 1/4 cup unsalted butter
- 1 cup mini marshmallows (store-bought or homemade)
- 1/2 cup chopped nuts (e.g., almonds, peanuts, or walnuts)
- 1/4 cup crispy rice cereal (optional)

Instructions:

1. Line an 8x8-inch pan with parchment paper.

2. Melt chocolate chips and butter in a double boiler or microwave until smooth.

3. Fold in marshmallows, nuts, and rice cereal (if using).

4. Pour the mixture into the prepared pan and spread evenly.

5. Refrigerate for 2–3 hours or until firm. Cut into bars and serve.

3. Honey Nougat

Honey nougat is a chewy, flavorful confection perfect for mixing with nuts and dried fruits.

Ingredients:

- 2 cups granulated sugar
- 1/2 cup honey
- 1/2 cup light corn syrup
- 1/4 cup water
- 2 large egg whites

- 1/2 teaspoon vanilla extract
- 1/4 teaspoon salt
- 1 cup toasted almonds or pistachios
- 1/2 cup dried cranberries or apricots (optional)

Instructions:

1. Line a loaf pan with parchment paper and grease lightly.

2. Combine sugar, honey, corn syrup, and water in a saucepan. Heat over medium heat, stirring until sugar dissolves.

3. Cook without stirring until the mixture reaches 248°F.

4. While the syrup is cooking, whip egg whites and salt in a stand mixer until stiff peaks form.

5. With the mixer on low, slowly pour the hot syrup into the egg whites.

6. Increase speed and whip until the mixture thickens and cools slightly (about 5–7 minutes).

7. Fold in nuts and dried fruits.

8. Pour the nougat into the prepared pan and smooth the top. Let set for 6 hours or overnight. Cut into pieces and wrap individually in wax paper.

Flavored and Colored Variations

1. Marshmallow Variations

- Flavors: Add extracts like peppermint, almond, or lemon for a twist.

- Colors: Use gel food coloring to create pastel or vibrant marshmallows. Swirl multiple colors for a marbled effect.

2. Nougat Variations

- Nutty Combinations: Use hazelnuts, cashews, or macadamia nuts for unique textures.

- Chocolate-Covered Nougat: Dip pieces in tempered chocolate for an indulgent treat.

3. Festive Designs

- Use cookie cutters to create themed marshmallows for holidays (e.g., hearts for Valentine's Day, stars for Christmas).

- Dust with edible glitter or colored sugar for an extra festive touch.

Troubleshooting Common Issues

1. Sticky Marshmallows

- Cause: Insufficient coating with powdered sugar and cornstarch.

- Solution: Liberally dust marshmallows after cutting and store in an airtight container.

2. Dense Nougat

- Cause: Overcooking sugar syrup or underwhipping egg whites.

- Solution: Monitor syrup temperature carefully and whip until stiff peaks form.

3. Lack of Flavor

- Cause: Insufficient flavoring.

- Solution: Use concentrated extracts or natural ingredients like citrus zest or spices.

Storage and Presentation

1. Marshmallows

- Store marshmallows in an airtight container at room temperature for up to two weeks.

- Package in cellophane bags with ribbons for gifting.

2. Nougat

- Wrap nougat pieces individually in wax or parchment paper to prevent sticking.

- Store in a cool, dry place for up to three weeks.

Creative Uses

- Marshmallow Hot Cocoa Stirrers: Place marshmallows on sticks and dip in chocolate for a fun addition to hot cocoa.

- Nougat Layer in Candy Bars: Use nougat as a layer in homemade candy bars, combining it with caramel or chocolate.

Conclusion

Marshmallows and nougat are confections that combine precision with creativity, offering endless opportunities for experimentation and customization. Whether crafting classic Vanilla Marshmallows, indulgent Rocky Road Bars, or nutty Honey Nougat, these recipes and techniques will help you master the art of light, airy sweets. With flavored and colored variations, you can create confections that suit any occasion, adding a personal touch to your candy-making repertoire. Let your imagination take flight as you explore the delicious world of marshmallows and nougat, turning simple ingredients into unforgettable treats.

Chapter 7: Brittle and Pralines

Crunchy, sweet, and satisfying, brittle and pralines are beloved confections that deliver a perfect blend of texture and flavor. These classic treats have stood the test of time, offering endless variations and customization options. Whether you're mastering the crack of a peanut brittle, the delicate sweetness of pralines, or the nutty simplicity of sesame snaps, achieving the ideal balance of caramelization, crunch, and flavor is an art worth perfecting. This chapter will guide you through the techniques for crafting flawless brittle and pralines, provide recipes for Peanut Brittle, Almond Pralines, and Sesame Snaps, and explore creative ways to add spices and seeds for unique twists.

Understanding Brittle and Pralines

1. What Is Brittle?

Brittle is a hard, flat confection made by cooking sugar to the hard crack stage and incorporating nuts, seeds, or other mix-ins. The result is a thin, crispy candy with a satisfying snap.

2. What Are Pralines?

Pralines are soft, buttery candies that combine caramelized sugar, cream or butter, and nuts. Their texture ranges from slightly crunchy to creamy, depending on the recipe and cooking technique.

3. Key Differences

- Texture: Brittle is hard and crisp, while pralines are softer and more melt-in-your-mouth.

- Ingredients: Brittle typically excludes dairy, focusing on sugar and nuts, whereas pralines include butter or cream for a rich, smooth consistency.

Perfecting the Art of Crunchy Confections

1. The Science of Sugar Stages

- Soft Ball Stage (235–240°F / 113–116°C): Used for creamy pralines.

- Hard Crack Stage (300°F / 150°C): Achieved when making brittle, ensuring a crisp texture.

2. Importance of Timing

- Overcooking results in a burnt taste, while undercooking leaves the candy sticky. Using a candy thermometer ensures precision.

3. Balancing Ingredients

- Sugar: Granulated sugar is the base for both brittle and pralines.

- Liquid Sweeteners: Corn syrup or honey prevents crystallization and enhances texture.

- Fat: Butter or cream adds richness to pralines.

- Nuts and Seeds: Provide flavor, texture, and visual appeal.

Techniques for Success

1. Preparing Ingredients

- Measure all ingredients before starting, as candy-making requires quick actions once the sugar reaches the correct stage.

- Toast nuts and seeds beforehand to enhance their flavor.

2. Cooking Sugar

- Use a heavy-bottomed saucepan for even heat distribution.

- Stir gently until sugar dissolves, then avoid stirring to prevent crystallization.

3. Using a Candy Thermometer

- Ensure the thermometer does not touch the bottom of the pan to avoid inaccurate readings.

- Monitor closely as sugar heats quickly near the hard crack stage.

4. Pouring and Setting

- Work quickly when pouring brittle onto a silicone mat or parchment paper, as it hardens rapidly.

- For pralines, spoon the mixture onto a prepared surface to create individual candies.

Recipes

1. Peanut Brittle

A timeless classic, peanut brittle combines the sweetness of caramelized sugar with the crunch of roasted peanuts.

Ingredients:

- 2 cups granulated sugar
- 1/2 cup light corn syrup
- 1/4 cup water
- 2 tablespoons unsalted butter
- 1/2 teaspoon baking soda
- 1 teaspoon vanilla extract
- 1 1/2 cups roasted peanuts

Instructions:

1. Line a baking sheet with a silicone mat or parchment paper.

2. Combine sugar, corn syrup, and water in a saucepan. Heat over medium heat, stirring until sugar dissolves.

3. Stop stirring and bring to a boil. Cook until the mixture reaches 300°F (hard crack stage).

4. Remove from heat and quickly stir in butter, baking soda, and vanilla. The mixture will foam.

5. Fold in peanuts and pour onto the prepared baking sheet, spreading evenly.

6. Let cool completely before breaking into pieces.

2. Almond Pralines

These buttery, nutty pralines melt in your mouth and are perfect for gifts or indulgent treats.

Ingredients:

- 1 cup granulated sugar
- 1/2 cup light brown sugar
- 1/2 cup heavy cream
- 1/4 cup unsalted butter
- 1/2 teaspoon salt
- 1 teaspoon vanilla extract
- 1 cup toasted almonds

Instructions:

1. Line a baking sheet with parchment paper.

2. Combine sugars, cream, butter, and salt in a saucepan. Heat over medium heat, stirring until sugar dissolves.

3. Cook to 240°F (soft ball stage), stirring occasionally.

4. Remove from heat and stir in vanilla and almonds.

5. Spoon the mixture onto the prepared baking sheet in small mounds.

6. Let cool completely before storing.

3. Sesame Snaps

These nutty, crunchy candies are simple to make and perfect for snacking.

Ingredients:

- 1 cup granulated sugar

- 1/4 cup honey

- 2 tablespoons water

- 1 cup toasted sesame seeds

- 1/4 teaspoon salt

Instructions:

1. Line a baking sheet with parchment paper or a silicone mat.

2. Combine sugar, honey, and water in a saucepan. Heat over medium heat, stirring until sugar dissolves.

3. Cook to 300°F (hard crack stage). Remove from heat and quickly stir in sesame seeds and salt.

4. Pour the mixture onto the prepared baking sheet and spread thinly.

5. Let cool completely before breaking into pieces.

Adding Spices and Seeds for Unique Twists

1. Spices

- Cinnamon and Nutmeg: Add warmth to pralines or brittle.

- Chili Powder: For a spicy-sweet kick in brittle.

2. Seeds

- Sunflower Seeds: Add to brittle for extra crunch and nuttiness.

- Poppy Seeds: Sprinkle over pralines for visual appeal and texture.

3. Herbs and Extracts

- Rosemary or Thyme: Infuse sugar syrup for a savory twist.

- Orange or Almond Extract: Complement nut-based confections.

Creative Presentation and Storage

1. Packaging

   - Wrap individual pieces in cellophane or parchment paper for gifting.

   - Arrange in decorative tins or boxes for a professional look.

   2. Storage

   - Store in an airtight container at room temperature to prevent brittleness from softening due to humidity.

   - Separate layers with parchment paper to avoid sticking.

Troubleshooting Common Issues

1. Grainy Brittle

   - Cause: Crystallization during cooking.

   - Solution: Use corn syrup or an acid like lemon juice to stabilize the sugar.

   2. Sticky Pralines

   - Cause: Under-cooking or high humidity.

   - Solution: Ensure the mixture reaches the correct temperature and store in a cool, dry place.

   3. Brittle Burning

   - Cause: Overheating the sugar syrup.

   - Solution: Monitor closely with a thermometer and remove from heat immediately at 300°F.

Incorporating Brittle and Pralines into Desserts

- Toppings: Crumble brittle or pralines over ice cream, yogurt, or cakes.

   - Mix-Ins: Chop and fold into cookie dough or brownie batter for added crunch.

   - Gift Ideas: Include brittle or pralines in homemade confectionery boxes alongside truffles and fudge.

Conclusion

Brittle and pralines are classic confections that combine the allure of caramelized sugar with the satisfying crunch of nuts and seeds. By mastering techniques like precise temperature control and creative flavoring, you can create treats that delight in both taste and texture. Whether crafting Peanut Brittle, Almond Pralines, or Sesame Snaps, these recipes offer a foundation for endless customization. Let your imagination guide you as you explore new spices, seeds, and presentation ideas, turning simple ingredients into unforgettable sweets. With a little practice, you'll be perfecting the art of crunchy confections in no time.

Chapter 8: Gummies and Jellies

Gummies and jellies are delightful confections that appeal to all ages. With their chewy texture and vibrant flavors, they bring a touch of fun and sophistication to the world of candy-making. The art of crafting gummies and jellies lies in mastering the balance of textures, flavors, and colors, achieved through the careful use of gelatin, pectin, and natural ingredients. This chapter explores the science of gummy and jelly-making, provides recipes for Fruit Gummies, Wine Gummies, and Turkish Delight, and discusses natural flavoring and coloring options to create unique, customized treats.

Understanding Gummies and Jellies

1. What Are Gummies?

Gummies are chewy candies made primarily from gelatin, sugar, and flavoring. Their elasticity and chewiness make them a favorite for both children and adults.

2. What Are Jellies?

Jellies are firmer, less elastic candies made using pectin or agar-agar. They have a softer bite and are often used for fruit-based candies.

3. Key Differences

- Gelling Agent: Gummies use gelatin for chewiness, while jellies rely on pectin or agar for a firmer texture.

- Texture: Gummies are elastic and chewy; jellies are smooth and tender.

- Flavors: Both can be flavored with fruit juices, extracts, or infusions.

The Science of Gelatin and Pectin-Based Candies

1. Gelatin

Gelatin is a protein derived from collagen that forms a gel-like structure when hydrated and cooled.

- Hydration: Gelatin must be bloomed in cold water before use to prevent clumping.

- Strength: The firmness of the gummies depends on the amount of gelatin used.

- Temperature Sensitivity: Gelatin melts at body temperature, giving gummies their characteristic melt-in-your-mouth texture.

2. Pectin

Pectin is a plant-based polysaccharide found in fruits, commonly used to thicken jellies and jams.

- Types of Pectin:

- High-Methoxyl Pectin: Requires sugar and acid to set, ideal for traditional jellies.

- Low-Methoxyl Pectin: Sets with calcium, suitable for low-sugar recipes.

- Usage: Pectin-based jellies are firmer and more stable than gelatin-based gummies.

Essential Tools and Ingredients

1. Tools

- Candy Thermometer: Ensures sugar reaches the correct temperature for setting.

- Silicone Molds: Perfect for shaping gummies and jellies into fun designs.

- Whisk and Saucepan: For mixing and heating ingredients evenly.

- Pipettes or Squeeze Bottles: Useful for precise filling of molds.

2. Ingredients

- Sugar: Provides sweetness and structure.

- Gelling Agents: Gelatin for gummies, pectin for jellies.

- Acid: Lemon juice or citric acid enhances flavor and helps jellies set.

- Natural Flavors: Fruit purees, juices, or extracts for authentic taste.

- Natural Colors: Derived from fruits, vegetables, or spices for vibrant hues.

Recipes

1. Fruit Gummies

These chewy, fruity treats are made with gelatin and natural fruit juice for a wholesome twist on classic gummies.

Ingredients:

- 1/2 cup fruit juice (e.g., orange, raspberry, or apple)
- 2 tablespoons honey or sugar
- 3 tablespoons unflavored gelatin
- 1 tablespoon lemon juice

Instructions:

1. Bloom gelatin by sprinkling it over 1/4 cup cold fruit juice. Let sit for 5 minutes.

2. Heat the remaining juice and honey in a saucepan over low heat until warm. Do not boil.

3. Add the bloomed gelatin to the warm juice, stirring until completely dissolved.

4. Stir in lemon juice.

5. Pour the mixture into silicone molds or a greased pan.

6. Refrigerate for 1–2 hours, or until set. Remove from molds or cut into shapes if using a pan.

2. Wine Gummies

Sophisticated and adult-friendly, these gummies incorporate wine for a refined flavor profile.

Ingredients:

- 1/2 cup red or white wine
- 2 tablespoons granulated sugar
- 2 tablespoons unflavored gelatin
- 1 teaspoon lemon juice

Instructions:

1. Bloom gelatin in 1/4 cup cold wine. Let sit for 5 minutes.

2. Heat the remaining wine and sugar in a saucepan over low heat until warm.

3. Stir in the bloomed gelatin until fully dissolved.

4. Add lemon juice for a touch of brightness.

5. Pour into silicone molds and refrigerate for 2 hours. Remove from molds and enjoy.

3. Turkish Delight

This classic Middle Eastern confection is a firmer jelly with a dusting of powdered sugar.

Ingredients:

- 2 cups granulated sugar

- 3/4 cup water

- 1/4 cup cornstarch

- 1 teaspoon lemon juice

- 1/2 teaspoon rosewater or orange blossom water

- 1/4 cup powdered sugar (for coating)

Instructions:

1. Combine sugar, water, and lemon juice in a saucepan. Heat over medium heat, stirring until sugar dissolves.

2. Boil the mixture until it reaches 240°F (soft ball stage).

3. In a separate bowl, mix cornstarch with 1/4 cup water to form a slurry. Add to the sugar mixture and whisk until thickened.

4. Remove from heat and stir in rosewater or orange blossom water.

5. Pour into a greased or parchment-lined pan. Let set for 4–6 hours.

6. Cut into squares and coat with powdered sugar.

Natural Flavoring and Coloring Options

1. Flavoring

- Fruits: Puree or juice from berries, citrus, or tropical fruits.

- Herbs and Spices: Mint, basil, or cinnamon for unique flavors.

- Extracts: Vanilla, almond, or coconut for added depth.

2. Coloring

- Beet Juice: For red or pink hues.

- Turmeric: Creates a warm yellow.

- Spinach or Matcha Powder: Adds green tones without overpowering flavors.

- Blueberry Juice: For natural blue or purple.

3. Tips for Balancing Flavor and Color

- Use concentrated juices or purees to avoid watering down the mixture.

- Combine complementary flavors and colors for a cohesive result.

Creative Variations

1. Multi-Layer Gummies

- Pour one flavor or color into molds, let it set slightly, then add another layer for a striped effect.

2. Sparkling Gummies

- Use sparkling wine or soda for a fizzy texture.

3. Themed Shapes

- Use molds in seasonal or themed designs, such as hearts for Valentine's Day or pumpkins for Halloween.

Troubleshooting Common Issues

1. Sticky Gummies or Jellies

- Cause: Insufficient cooling or high humidity.

- Solution: Dust with cornstarch or powdered sugar before storing.

2. Soft or Runny Texture

- Cause: Undercooked sugar syrup or incorrect gelling agent ratio.

- Solution: Cook syrup to the correct temperature and measure ingredients precisely.

3. Cloudy Appearance

- Cause: Impurities or over-stirring during cooking.

- Solution: Use clear juice or strain mixtures before setting.

Storage and Presentation

1. Storage

- Store gummies and jellies in an airtight container at room temperature for up to two weeks.

- Separate layers with parchment paper to prevent sticking.

2. Presentation

- Package in clear bags tied with ribbons for gifting.

- Arrange in decorative boxes with compartments for different flavors.

Conclusion

Gummies and jellies are versatile, playful confections that bring a burst of color and flavor to any occasion. By mastering the art of gelatin and pectin-based candies, you can create treats that range from simple fruit gummies to elegant Turkish Delight. With natural flavoring and coloring options, the possibilities for customization are endless, allowing you to tailor each batch to your tastes and preferences. Whether you're crafting them for fun, gifting, or as a creative culinary project, gummies and jellies are sure to delight both the maker and the recipient. Let your imagination run wild as you explore this sweet and satisfying world.

Chapter 9: Confectionery for Special Diets

Confectionery for special diets is no longer a niche but a growing necessity in today's world of diverse dietary needs. Whether you're catering to individuals avoiding sugar, following plant-based lifestyles, or adhering to gluten-free regimens, crafting sweets that fit these requirements can be both a creative challenge and a rewarding endeavor. With the right knowledge of alternative ingredients and techniques, it's possible to create indulgent confections that satisfy dietary restrictions without sacrificing flavor or texture. This chapter explores the art of making sugar-free, vegan, and gluten-free sweets, shares recipes for Keto Caramel, Vegan Marshmallows, and Fruit Leather, and provides tips for using alternative sweeteners and thickeners effectively.

The Foundations of Special Diet Confectionery

1. Understanding Dietary Restrictions

- Sugar-Free: Eliminates refined sugars, often using natural or artificial sweeteners.
  - Vegan: Avoids all animal-derived ingredients, including gelatin, dairy, and honey.
  - Gluten-Free: Excludes gluten-containing grains like wheat, barley, and rye.

2. Common Challenges

- Replicating sweetness and texture without refined sugar.
  - Achieving elasticity and firmness without gelatin.
  - Creating structure and consistency in gluten-free recipes.

3. Key Ingredients

- Sweeteners: Stevia, erythritol, monk fruit, maple syrup, and coconut sugar.
  - Thickeners: Agar-agar, pectin, arrowroot powder, and xanthan gum.
  - Binding Agents: Flaxseed meal, chia seeds, aquafaba (chickpea water).

Making Sugar-Free Confections

1. Sweetener Options

- Stevia: A plant-derived sweetener, highly concentrated and calorie-free.
    - Erythritol: A sugar alcohol with a cooling effect, suitable for baking and candy.
    - Monk Fruit Sweetener: Naturally derived with a clean, sweet flavor and zero calories.

2. Tips for Success

- Adjust recipes carefully, as alternative sweeteners often have different sweetness levels than sugar.
    - Combine multiple sweeteners to mimic the flavor and mouthfeel of sugar.
    - Add a pinch of salt or an acid (like lemon juice) to balance sweetness.

Recipe: Keto Caramel

This sugar-free caramel is rich, buttery, and perfect for drizzling over desserts or using in candies.

Ingredients:
- 1/2 cup erythritol or allulose
- 1/4 cup unsalted butter (or vegan butter for plant-based)
- 1/4 cup heavy cream (or coconut cream for plant-based)
- 1/2 teaspoon vanilla extract
- Pinch of salt

Instructions:

1. Melt butter in a saucepan over medium heat. Add erythritol and stir until dissolved.

2. Slowly add cream, stirring continuously. Cook until the mixture thickens and turns golden brown (about 5–7 minutes).

3. Remove from heat and stir in vanilla extract and salt.

4. Let cool slightly before using. Store in an airtight container in the refrigerator for up to two weeks.

Crafting Vegan Confections

1. Replacing Gelatin

- Agar-Agar: A seaweed-based gelling agent that mimics gelatin's structure.
    - Pecti: Ideal for jellies and chewy candies.
    - Aquafaba: Whipped chickpea water that serves as a substitute for egg whites.

2. Vegan Alternatives

- Dairy-Free Milk: Almond, oat, or coconut milk for creaminess.
    - Plant-Based Butter: Coconut oil or vegan butter for richness.
    - Natural Sweeteners: Maple syrup, agave, or date syrup.

Recipe: Vegan Marshmallows

Soft, fluffy, and perfect for toasting, these marshmallows are entirely plant-based.

Ingredients:
- 1 cup granulated sugar
- 1/2 cup light corn syrup or agave syrup
- 1/2 cup water
- 2 teaspoons agar-agar powder
- 1/2 cup aquafaba
- 1/4 teaspoon cream of tartar
- 1 teaspoon vanilla extract
- Powdered sugar and cornstarch for dusting

Instructions:

1. Combine sugar, corn syrup, and water in a saucepan. Heat over medium heat until the mixture reaches 240°F.

2. In a small bowl, dissolve agar-agar in 1/4 cup water and simmer for 2–3 minutes until thickened.

3. In a stand mixer, whip aquafaba and cream of tartar until stiff peaks form.

4. Slowly pour the hot syrup and agar-agar mixture into the whipped aquafaba, beating continuously.

5. Add vanilla extract and beat until the mixture thickens and cools slightly.

6. Pour into a greased and dusted pan, smooth the top, and let set for 4–6 hours.

7. Cut into squares and coat with powdered sugar and cornstarch mixture.

Creating Gluten-Free Confections

1. Gluten-Free Flours

- Almond Flour: Adds nuttiness and moisture.
    - Coconut Flour: Absorbs liquid, ideal for dense confections.
    - Rice Flour: A versatile base for gluten-free recipes.

2. Binding Agents

- Xanthan Gum: Provides elasticity and structure.
    - Flaxseed or Chia Seeds: Hydrated seeds act as a binding agent.

Recipe: Fruit Leather

This naturally gluten-free and vegan treat is a chewy, flavorful snack made with fresh fruit.

Ingredients:
- 3 cups fresh or frozen fruit (e.g., strawberries, mangoes, or apples)
- 1/4 cup honey or maple syrup (optional)
- 1 tablespoon lemon juice

Instructions:

1. Preheat oven to 170°F (or the lowest setting). Line a baking sheet with parchment paper.

2. Blend fruit, sweetener, and lemon juice in a blender until smooth.

3. Pour the puree onto the prepared baking sheet and spread evenly.

4. Bake for 4–6 hours, or until the mixture is dry but still pliable.

5. Let cool, then cut into strips and roll with parchment paper for storage.

Tips for Using Alternative Ingredients

1. Sweeteners

- Blending Sweeteners: Combine erythritol with stevia or monk fruit to reduce aftertaste.

- Adjusting Ratios: Use slightly more liquid sweeteners (like maple syrup) to maintain moisture balance.

2. Thickeners

- Agar-Agar: Requires boiling to activate and set.

- Pectin: Needs sugar and acid for proper gelling.

3. Flavor Balancing

- Counteract bitterness from artificial sweeteners with a touch of salt or acid.

- Use natural extracts and spices to enhance depth.

Troubleshooting Common Issues

1. Grainy Texture

- Cause: Undissolved sweeteners.

- Solution: Heat mixtures gently and stir until completely dissolved.

2. Insufficient Setting

- Cause: Incorrect ratios of gelling agents.

- Solution: Measure thickeners precisely and ensure proper cooking temperatures.

3. Overly Sweet Flavor

- Cause: Overcompensating with alternative sweeteners.

- Solution: Use a blend of sweeteners and balance with acidic ingredients.

Creative Presentation and Storage

1. Packaging

- Use resealable pouches for fruit leather.

- Arrange marshmallows or keto caramels in decorative tins for gifting.

2. Storage

- Store sugar-free and gluten-free confections in airtight containers at room temperature.

- Keep vegan marshmallows in the refrigerator to maintain freshness.

Conclusion

Creating confectionery for special diets is a rewarding way to bring sweetness to everyone's life, regardless of dietary restrictions. By mastering the use of alternative sweeteners, thickeners, and flours, you can craft indulgent treats like Keto Caramel, Vegan Marshmallows, and Fruit Leather that rival traditional sweets in flavor and texture. These recipes and tips provide a foundation for endless experimentation, allowing you to customize confections to suit specific needs and preferences. Whether for personal enjoyment or to delight others, these inclusive confections prove that dietary restrictions are no barrier to delicious creativity.

Chapter 10: International Confections

The world of confectionery is as diverse and rich as the cultures that inspire it. Across the globe, candy-making traditions reflect local ingredients, techniques, and celebrations, offering a glimpse into the cultural heart of each region. From the airy sweetness of French Nougat to the chewy delight of Japanese Mochi and the syrup-soaked indulgence of Indian Jalebi, exploring international confections is a journey of flavor, texture, and artistry. This chapter delves into the history and techniques behind these global sweets, provides detailed recipes, and offers tips for adapting traditional methods to the modern home kitchen.

The Global Appeal of Confections

1. Cultural Significance

Confections are deeply tied to traditions and celebrations:

- Festivals and Ceremonies: Many sweets are central to religious festivals, weddings, and other milestone events.

- Symbolism: Candies often symbolize prosperity, happiness, or blessings in various cultures.

2. Regional Influences

The flavors and techniques of confections are shaped by geography:

- Europe: Emphasis on refined sugarwork, chocolates, and nougat.

- Asia: Use of rice, beans, and natural flavorings like matcha and sesame.

- Middle East and India: Focus on syrup-soaked sweets, nuts, and aromatic spices.

French Nougat

1. Background

Nougat, or "nougat de Montélimar," is a classic French candy made with whipped egg whites, honey, sugar, and nuts. Its origins trace back to the Mediterranean, where almonds and honey were abundant.

2. Texture and Variations

- Soft Nougat: Chewy and airy, perfect for bars and candies.

- Hard Nougat: Crisp and brittle, often combined with chocolate or caramel.

Recipe: Classic French Nougat

Ingredients:
- 2 cups granulated sugar
- 1/2 cup honey
- 1/2 cup light corn syrup
- 1/4 cup water
- 2 large egg whites
- 1/2 teaspoon vanilla extract
- 1/4 teaspoon salt
- 1 cup toasted almonds
- 1/2 cup pistachios

Instructions:

1. Line a loaf pan with parchment paper and grease lightly.

2. Combine sugar, honey, corn syrup, and water in a saucepan. Heat over medium heat, stirring until sugar dissolves.

3. Continue cooking without stirring until the mixture reaches 248°F (firm ball stage).

4. Meanwhile, whip egg whites and salt in a stand mixer until stiff peaks form.

5. Slowly pour the hot syrup into the egg whites while beating on low speed.

6. Increase speed and whip until the mixture thickens and cools slightly. Stir in vanilla and nuts.

7. Pour into the prepared pan and smooth the top. Let set for 6 hours or overnight.

8. Cut into pieces and wrap individually in wax paper.

Japanese Mochi

1. Background

Mochi is a traditional Japanese confection made from glutinous rice that is pounded into a sticky, elastic dough. It is often filled with sweetened bean paste or flavored with natural ingredients like matcha or fruit.

2. Cultural Context

Mochi is a staple during *Japanese New Year* celebrations and is also used in desserts like *daifuku* (mochi filled with sweet fillings) and *ice cream mochi*.

Recipe: Homemade Matcha Mochi

Ingredients:
- 1 cup glutinous rice flour (mochiko)
- 1/4 cup granulated sugar
- 3/4 cup water
- 1 teaspoon matcha powder
- Cornstarch or potato starch (for dusting)

Instructions:

1. Mix rice flour, sugar, water, and matcha powder in a microwave-safe bowl until smooth.

2. Microwave the mixture on high for 2 minutes. Stir and microwave for another minute until thick and sticky.

3. Dust a surface with cornstarch and transfer the dough onto it. Let cool slightly.

4. Cut the dough into pieces and flatten each piece into a disc. Fill with sweetened bean paste or another filling of choice, then pinch the edges to seal.

5. Roll in cornstarch to prevent sticking. Serve fresh.

Indian Jalebi

1. Background

Jalebi is a popular Indian sweet made by deep-frying fermented batter into spirals and soaking them in saffron-infused sugar syrup. Known for its crispy texture and syrupy sweetness, jalebi is enjoyed during festivals and celebrations.

2. Variations
- Imarti: A similar sweet made with urad dal (black gram) batter.
- Rabri Jalebi: Served with thickened sweetened milk for added richness.

Recipe: Traditional Jalebi

Ingredients:

For the Batter:

- 1 cup all-purpose flour

- 2 tablespoons cornstarch

- 1/4 teaspoon turmeric powder (for color)

- 1/2 teaspoon yeast or 1/4 teaspoon baking powder

- 1/2 cup water

For the Syrup:

- 1 cup sugar

- 1/2 cup water

- 1/4 teaspoon cardamom powder

- A pinch of saffron strands

Instructions:

1. Combine flour, cornstarch, turmeric, and yeast in a bowl. Add water to make a thick batter. Cover and let ferment for 1–2 hours.

2. Prepare the syrup by heating sugar and water in a saucepan. Simmer until slightly thickened. Add cardamom and saffron. Keep warm.

3. Heat oil in a deep pan. Transfer the batter to a piping bag or squeeze bottle.

4. Pipe the batter into the oil in spiral shapes. Fry until golden and crisp.

5. Dip the fried jalebis into the warm syrup for 30 seconds. Remove and serve warm or at room temperature.

Adapting Traditional Techniques for Home Kitchens

1. Simplifying Equipment

- Replace traditional stone mortars for mochi pounding with stand mixers.

- Use squeeze bottles for jalebi instead of piping cloths for easier handling.

2. Ingredient Substitutions

- Substitute hard-to-find nuts or spices with locally available options (e.g., pecans for pistachios in nougat).

- Use agar-agar as a vegetarian alternative to gelatin in mochi fillings.

3. Small Batch Sizes

- Scale down recipes to accommodate home kitchen equipment and avoid waste.

Natural Flavoring and Coloring

1. Nougat
    - Infuse honey with lavender or rosemary for unique flavors.
    - Add dried fruits like apricots or cranberries for natural sweetness and color.
    2. Mochi
    - Use purees from strawberries, mangoes, or yuzu for vibrant colors and authentic flavors.
    - Incorporate matcha, cocoa powder, or sesame for natural color and taste.
    3. Jalebi
    - Replace saffron with turmeric or natural food dyes for a budget-friendly alternative.
    - Experiment with floral syrups like rose or orange blossom.

Creative Serving Ideas

- Nougat: Serve with coffee or tea on a decorative platter for an elegant dessert.
    - Mochi: Pair with green tea ice cream or drizzle with sweetened condensed milk.
    - Jalebi: Serve with rabri (sweetened milk) or yogurt for a traditional Indian breakfast treat.

Troubleshooting Common Issues

1. Sticky Nougat
    - Cause: Insufficient whipping or high humidity.
    - Solution: Ensure the sugar syrup reaches the correct temperature and store nougat in wax paper.
    2. Hard Mochi
    - Cause: Overcooking the dough.

- Solution: Steam the dough instead of microwaving for better texture control.

3. Soggy Jalebi

- Cause: Over-soaking in syrup.

- Solution: Dip jalebis briefly and allow excess syrup to drip off before serving.

Conclusion

International confections like French Nougat, Japanese Mochi, and Indian Jalebi reflect the unique cultural heritage of their origins while offering endless opportunities for creativity and adaptation. By exploring these sweets, you not only expand your confectionery skills but also connect with traditions and flavors from around the globe. With the recipes and techniques shared in this chapter, you can recreate these beloved confections in your home kitchen, adding your own twists to make them uniquely yours. Let these global treats inspire your confectionery journey, celebrating diversity and sweetness in every bite.

Chapter 11: Confectionery for Gifting

Homemade confectionery is one of the most thoughtful and delightful gifts you can give. Crafted with care and presented beautifully, candies and sweets become more than just a treat—they become a gesture of love, creativity, and personal touch. Whether it's an assortment of handmade chocolates, colorful edible ornaments for the holidays, or chocolate-covered pretzels for a party favor, confectionery gifts are suitable for every occasion. This chapter explores how to package and present homemade candies as gifts, shares recipes for Assorted Gift Boxes, Chocolate-Covered Pretzels, and Edible Ornaments, and offers ideas for creating seasonal and themed treats that captivate and delight.

The Art of Gifting Confectionery

1. Why Confectionery Makes the Perfect Gift

- Universal Appeal: Almost everyone enjoys sweets, making them a versatile gift.
- Personal Touch: Homemade candies convey effort, thoughtfulness, and care.
- Customizable: Confections can be tailored to suit tastes, dietary preferences, or special occasions.

2. Key Considerations for Gifting

- Shelf Life: Choose confections that maintain freshness over time, such as hard candies, brittles, and truffles.
- Allergy Awareness: Consider common allergens like nuts, dairy, or gluten when selecting or labeling your gifts.
- Presentation: Eye-catching packaging enhances the experience and adds to the gift's appeal.

Packaging and Presenting Homemade Candies

1. Essential Packaging Materials

- Boxes and Tins: Ideal for assorted chocolates, truffles, and cookies. Choose decorative designs for seasonal themes.

- Cellophane Bags: Perfect for smaller treats like hard candies, caramels, or chocolate-covered pretzels.

- Jars: Suitable for gifting layered candy mixes, brittle, or colorful candies like gummies.

- Wax Paper or Parchment: For wrapping individual candies such as nougats, caramels, or fudge.

- Ribbons and Tags: Add a finishing touch with decorative ribbons, bows, and personalized gift tags.

2. Creative Presentation Ideas

- Themed Gift Boxes: Arrange candies by flavor, color, or type, such as a "chocolate lover's collection" or "spiced holiday treats."

- Layered Jars: Layer different colors or types of candies in glass jars for a visually appealing gift.

- Seasonal Designs: Incorporate seasonal elements, like snowflake patterns for winter or pastel hues for spring.

3. Tips for Professional Presentation

- Use food-safe materials to protect candies from contamination.

- Arrange candies neatly in compartments or layers, using separators to prevent sticking.

- Add a personal note or recipe card for an extra-special touch.

Recipes for Gifting

1. Assorted Gift Boxes

An assortment of homemade candies makes for a luxurious and versatile gift. This recipe offers three varieties: chocolate truffles, peanut butter cups, and peppermint bark.

Chocolate Truffles

Ingredients:

- 8 oz dark chocolate, finely chopped
- 1/2 cup heavy cream
- 1 teaspoon vanilla extract
- Cocoa powder, chopped nuts, or sprinkles for coating

Instructions:

1. Heat cream in a saucepan until just simmering. Pour over chopped chocolate and let sit for 2 minutes. Stir until smooth.

2. Add vanilla extract and mix. Refrigerate for 1–2 hours until firm.

3. Scoop teaspoon-sized portions, roll into balls, and coat with cocoa powder, nuts, or sprinkles.

Peanut Butter Cups

Ingredients:

- 1 cup semisweet chocolate chips
- 1/2 cup peanut butter
- 2 tablespoons powdered sugar

Instructions:

1. Melt chocolate chips in a microwave or double boiler.

2. Mix peanut butter with powdered sugar.

3. Spoon a layer of melted chocolate into mini cupcake liners, add a dollop of peanut butter mixture, and top with more chocolate. Refrigerate until set.

Peppermint Bark

Ingredients:
- 8 oz white chocolate, melted
- 1/2 cup crushed peppermint candies

Instructions:

1. Spread melted white chocolate onto a parchment-lined baking sheet.

2. Sprinkle crushed peppermint candies over the top. Let set in the refrigerator before breaking into pieces.

2. Chocolate-Covered Pretzels

These sweet-and-salty treats are easy to make and endlessly customizable.

Ingredients:
- 1 bag of pretzel rods or twists
- 8 oz semisweet or milk chocolate, melted
- Optional toppings: sprinkles, chopped nuts, crushed candies

Instructions:

1. Dip pretzels halfway into melted chocolate, letting excess drip off.

2. Place on a parchment-lined baking sheet. Sprinkle with toppings before the chocolate sets.

3. Let set at room temperature or refrigerate until firm.

Variations:
- Drizzle with white or dark chocolate for a decorative effect.
- Use colorful sprinkles for a festive look.

3. Edible Ornaments

Perfect for holidays, these decorative candies double as tree ornaments and delicious treats.

Ingredients:
- 2 cups granulated sugar
- 2/3 cup light corn syrup
- 1/4 cup water
- Gel food coloring
- Candy flavoring (optional)

- Ribbon or string for hanging

Instructions:

1. Combine sugar, corn syrup, and water in a saucepan. Heat over medium heat, stirring until sugar dissolves.

2. Boil without stirring until the mixture reaches 300°F (hard crack stage).

3. Remove from heat and add food coloring and flavoring. Stir gently.

4. Pour the mixture into greased cookie cutters or silicone molds. Insert a small hole at the top with a skewer for the ribbon.

5. Let cool completely, then remove from molds and thread ribbons through the holes.

Ideas for Seasonal and Themed Treats

1. Seasonal Treats

- Winter: Peppermint bark, spiced truffles, or snowflake-shaped hard candies.
- Spring: Floral gummies, pastel-colored marshmallows, or lemon-flavored fudge.
- Summer: Tropical fruit leathers, citrus caramels, or ice cream-inspired chocolates.
- Autumn: Pumpkin spice truffles, caramel apples, or cinnamon bark.

2. Themed Treats

- Holidays: Heart-shaped chocolates for Valentine's Day or star-shaped candies for Independence Day.
- Birthdays: Customized candies in the recipient's favorite flavors or colors.
- Weddings and Showers: Monogrammed truffles or candies that match the event's color scheme.

3. Edible Decorations

- Candy canes or peppermint sticks for holiday tree décor.
- Sugar cookies decorated with royal icing as edible placeholders for parties.

Storage and Shelf Life

1. Proper Storage

- Store candies in airtight containers to prevent moisture or staleness.

- Keep away from direct sunlight and extreme temperatures.

2. Shelf Life

- Hard candies and brittles: Up to 6 months if stored in a cool, dry place.

- Truffles and fudge: 2–3 weeks in the refrigerator.

- Chocolate-covered treats: 1–2 weeks at room temperature or longer in the refrigerator.

Tips for Efficient Candy Production

1. Plan Ahead

- Make candies in batches and store them ahead of time to reduce last-minute stress.

2. Streamline Processes

- Use molds and cutters for uniform shapes.

- Invest in a candy thermometer to ensure consistent results.

3. Get Creative

- Experiment with flavors, colors, and designs to create unique gifts.

Conclusion

Confectionery for gifting combines the joy of homemade treats with the delight of sharing your creativity and care. Whether you're assembling Assorted Gift Boxes, crafting Chocolate-Covered Pretzels, or creating festive Edible Ornaments, the possibilities are endless. By focusing on thoughtful presentation, seasonal inspiration, and personalized touches, you can transform simple sweets into memorable gifts for any occasion. Let your imagination guide you as you explore the art of gifting confectionery, creating moments of sweetness that your loved ones will cherish.

Chapter 12: Confectionery for Kids

Confectionery for kids is all about fun, color, and creativity. Children love sweets that are vibrant and exciting, and even more so when they can participate in making them. Crafting homemade candies with kids is a wonderful way to bond, teach kitchen skills, and encourage creativity. From assembling candy necklaces to crafting colorful marshmallows and experimenting with fizzy, popping candy, there's no limit to the enjoyment. However, safety is paramount when working with children in the kitchen, especially when handling hot sugar or small edible pieces. This chapter provides recipes for Candy Necklaces, Rainbow Marshmallows, and Pop Rocks-style Fizzy Candy, along with practical safety tips for a joyful and safe confectionery experience.

The Joy of Making Candy with Kids

1. Why Make Candy with Kids?

- Creative Expression: Kids love to express themselves through vibrant colors, shapes, and designs.

  - Skill Building: Candy-making helps develop fine motor skills, math (measuring ingredients), and patience.

  - Memorable Moments: Shared kitchen experiences create lasting memories.

2. Key Considerations

- Age-Appropriate Tasks: Assign tasks based on the child's age and abilities. For example, younger children can mix or decorate, while older kids can assist with measuring and assembly.

  - Focus on Simplicity: Choose recipes with manageable steps to keep kids engaged.

  - Celebrate Creativity: Encourage kids to experiment with colors, shapes, and decorations.

Safety Tips for Working with Kids in the Kitchen

1. Supervision

- Always supervise children, especially when working near hot surfaces, sharp tools, or boiling sugar.

2. Heat Awareness

- Explain the dangers of hot pans, stoves, and boiling sugar. Assign tasks that keep kids away from heat sources.

3. Safe Tools

- Use kid-friendly tools such as plastic knives, silicone molds, and mixing bowls with rubber bottoms for stability.

4. Small Parts

- Avoid using small, hard candies or beads for very young children to prevent choking hazards.

5. Cleanliness

- Teach kids to wash hands thoroughly before and after handling food. Keep surfaces clean to prevent cross-contamination.

6. Emergency Preparedness

- Keep a first aid kit handy and know basic burn care techniques.

Recipes

1. Candy Necklaces

Candy necklaces are a nostalgic treat that doubles as a fun craft project. Kids can thread colorful candies onto string to create edible jewelry.

Ingredients:

- Assorted hard candies with holes (e.g., Life Savers) or candy beads
- String or thin elastic cord (food-safe)

Instructions:

1. Cut the string or elastic cord to the desired length, leaving extra for tying.
2. Tie a knot at one end to prevent candies from sliding off.
3. Let kids thread candies onto the string, creating patterns or designs.
4. Once filled, tie the ends together to form a necklace.

Tips:

- Use a blunt needle or toothpick to widen candy holes if needed.
- Incorporate marshmallows or gummy candies for variety.

2. Rainbow Marshmallows

These vibrant marshmallows are a colorful twist on a classic treat, perfect for snacking or decorating desserts.

Ingredients:
- 1/2 cup cold water
- 3 packets unflavored gelatin (about 7.5 teaspoons)
- 2 cups granulated sugar
- 1/2 cup light corn syrup
- 1/4 teaspoon salt
- 1 teaspoon vanilla extract
- Gel food coloring (various colors)
- Powdered sugar and cornstarch for dusting

Instructions:
1. Line a 9x13-inch pan with parchment paper and dust with a mixture of powdered sugar and cornstarch.
2. Bloom gelatin by sprinkling it over cold water in a stand mixer bowl.
3. Combine sugar, corn syrup, and 1/4 cup water in a saucepan. Heat over medium heat until the mixture reaches 240°F.
4. Slowly pour the hot syrup into the gelatin while whipping on low speed. Gradually increase speed and whip until thick and fluffy (about 10 minutes).
5. Divide the marshmallow mixture into separate bowls and tint each with a different color.
6. Layer the colored mixtures in the prepared pan, spreading evenly.
7. Let set for 6 hours or overnight. Cut into cubes or shapes and dust with powdered sugar mixture.

Tips:
- Use cookie cutters to create fun shapes.
- Let kids mix and match colors for a marbled effect.

3. Pop Rocks-Style Fizzy Candy

This DIY version of fizzy candy is a fun science experiment that kids will love.

Ingredients:

- 2 cups granulated sugar
- 1/2 cup light corn syrup
- 1/4 cup water
- 1 teaspoon citric acid
- 1/2 teaspoon baking soda
- Gel food coloring (optional)
- Flavoring extracts (e.g., strawberry, lemon)

Instructions:

1. Line a baking sheet with parchment paper or a silicone mat.

2. Combine sugar, corn syrup, and water in a saucepan. Heat over medium heat, stirring until sugar dissolves.

3. Boil the mixture until it reaches 300°F (hard crack stage). Remove from heat.

4. Stir in citric acid, baking soda, food coloring, and flavoring. The mixture will foam slightly.

5. Pour onto the prepared baking sheet and spread thinly.

6. Once hardened, break into small pieces and store in an airtight container.

Tips:

- Let kids watch the candy foam to learn about chemical reactions.
- Use multiple colors and flavors for variety.

Seasonal and Themed Treats

1. Seasonal Ideas

- Winter: Snowflake-shaped marshmallows, peppermint bark necklaces.
    - Spring: Pastel-colored gummies, flower-shaped candies.
    - Summer: Tropical fruit leather or gummy fish.
    - Autumn: Caramel apples, pumpkin spice marshmallows.

2. Themed Treats

- Birthdays: Use number-shaped molds or customize with the child's favorite colors.

- Holidays: Heart-shaped candies for Valentine's Day, jack-o'-lantern gummies for Halloween.
- Parties: Create candy kabobs or edible wands with marshmallows and sprinkles.

Encouraging Creativity

1. Decorating Candies
   - Provide sprinkles, edible glitter, or icing pens for kids to personalize their creations.
   - Let them "paint" marshmallows with edible food colors.
   2. Mixing Flavors
   - Experiment with fruit purees, extracts, or spices to create unique combinations.
   3. Building Structures
   - Use candies to build edible sculptures, such as candy houses or marshmallow towers.

Storage and Gifting

1. Storage Tips
   - Store candies in airtight containers to maintain freshness.
   - Use parchment paper between layers to prevent sticking.
   2. Gifting Ideas
   - Pack candies in colorful cellophane bags tied with ribbons.
   - Create personalized gift boxes with the child's name or designs.

Troubleshooting Common Issues

1. Sticky Candies
   - Cause: Humidity or insufficient dusting with powdered sugar.
   - Solution: Dust with extra powdered sugar or store in a cool, dry place.
   2. Marshmallow Layers Mixing
   - Cause: Layers not set before adding the next color.

- Solution: Let each layer firm up slightly before adding the next.

3. Hard or Burnt Candy

- Cause: Overcooking sugar syrup.

- Solution: Use a candy thermometer and monitor temperature closely.

Conclusion

Making confectionery with kids is a magical experience that combines creativity, learning, and fun. Whether threading candy necklaces, crafting colorful marshmallows, or experimenting with fizzy candies, these projects are sure to bring smiles and laughter to the kitchen. With the right safety precautions, simple recipes, and a dash of imagination, you can create not only delicious treats but also cherished memories. Let this chapter inspire you to explore the joy of candy-making with children, one sweet creation at a time.

Chapter 13: Advanced Techniques in Confectionery

Confectionery is an art form that allows for endless creativity and precision. While mastering basic recipes and techniques is essential, advanced confectionery techniques elevate candies and decorations to the level of edible art. From working with isomalt for intricate sugar sculptures to creating delicate edible lace and spun sugar, these methods require skill, patience, and the right tools. Adding the final flourish with airbrushing and edible glitter can transform your creations into stunning masterpieces. This chapter explores advanced techniques in confectionery, provides recipes for Sugar Sculptures, Edible Lace, and Spun Sugar, and offers guidance on mastering finishing touches like airbrushing and edible glitter.

The Art of Advanced Confectionery

1. What Is Advanced Confectionery?

Advanced confectionery involves precision techniques, specialized ingredients, and decorative artistry to craft professional-quality edible creations.

2. Key Skills in Advanced Confectionery

- Understanding the chemistry of sugar work and achieving the right temperature for specific effects.

- Mastering specialized tools like molds, airbrushes, and sugar pumps.

- Learning how to balance aesthetics with structural integrity.

3. Essential Tools and Equipment

- Candy Thermometer: Ensures accurate temperature control for sugar work.

- Silicone Mats and Molds: For shaping and setting sugar creations.

- Heat Lamps: Keeps sugar pliable while working.

- Airbrush Machine: For applying edible colors with precision.

- Edible Glitter and Dusts: Adds sparkle and elegance to decorations.

Working with Isomalt

Isomalt, a sugar substitute derived from beet sugar, is a key ingredient for advanced sugar work. Its stability and clarity make it ideal for creating intricate decorations.

1. Why Use Isomalt?

- Heat Stability: Less prone to crystallization than regular sugar.

- Clarity: Produces a glass-like finish, perfect for sculptures and decorations.

- Versatility: Can be molded, pulled, or blown into various shapes.

2. Tips for Working with Isomalt

- Use a candy thermometer to heat isomalt to 320°F (160°C) for optimal workability.

- Wear heat-resistant gloves to handle hot isomalt safely.

- Work in a dry environment, as humidity can affect the texture and stability of isomalt creations.

Recipes

1. Sugar Sculptures

Sugar sculptures are impressive showpieces that can be used as cake toppers or centerpiece decorations.

Ingredients:

- 2 cups isomalt powder

- 1/2 cup water

- Gel food coloring (optional)

Instructions:

1. Combine isomalt powder and water in a saucepan. Heat over medium heat, stirring gently until dissolved.

2. Increase heat and cook until the mixture reaches 320°F (hard crack stage). Remove from heat.

3. If desired, add a few drops of gel food coloring and stir gently.

4. Pour the hot isomalt onto a silicone mat or into molds. Let cool slightly until pliable.

5. Shape the isomalt into desired forms using silicone gloves or tools.

6. Allow the sculpture to cool completely before handling.

Tips:

- Use sugar pumps to create blown sugar spheres for added dimensions.

- Combine multiple colors for a marbled effect.

2. Edible Lace

Edible lace adds an elegant, intricate touch to cakes, cookies, and desserts.

Ingredients:

- 1/4 cup isomalt powder

- 1/4 cup water

- Food-safe silicone lace mat

Instructions:

1. Combine isomalt powder and water in a saucepan. Heat over medium heat until dissolved.

2. Pour the mixture onto the silicone lace mat, spreading evenly with an offset spatula.

3. Allow the isomalt to set for a few minutes, then gently peel it from the mat.

4. Trim edges as needed and use immediately or store in an airtight container.

Tips:

- Add a touch of edible glitter for a shimmering effect.

- Create colored lace by adding gel food coloring to the isomalt mixture.

3. Spun Sugar

Spun sugar is a delicate, web-like decoration that adds drama and elegance to desserts.

Ingredients:

- 2 cups granulated sugar

- 1/2 cup water

- 1/4 cup light corn syrup

Instructions:

1. Combine sugar, water, and corn syrup in a saucepan. Heat over medium heat, stirring until the sugar dissolves.

2. Increase heat and cook until the mixture reaches 310°F (hard crack stage). Remove from heat and let cool slightly.

3. Dip a fork or whisk into the sugar syrup and quickly flick it back and forth over a silicone mat or parchment paper to create thin, thread-like strands.

4. Gather the strands into nests or shapes and use immediately.

Tips:

- Work quickly, as the sugar will harden as it cools.

- Store spun sugar in a dry, airtight container to prevent melting.

Mastering Airbrushing

Airbrushing is a professional technique used to apply edible colors smoothly and precisely to confections.

1. Choosing an Airbrush Machine

- Select a machine with adjustable pressure settings for greater control.

- Use food-safe, liquid airbrush colors for best results.

2. Techniques

- Gradients: Blend colors smoothly by adjusting the distance and pressure of the airbrush.

- Stencils: Use food-safe stencils to create intricate patterns or designs.

- Highlighting: Add depth and dimension by layering colors or applying metallic tones.

3. Tips for Success

- Practice on parchment paper before applying to confections.

- Clean the airbrush thoroughly after each use to prevent clogging.

- Use light, even strokes to avoid oversaturation.

Using Edible Glitter and Dust

Edible glitter and dusts add sparkle and elegance to your confectionery creations, making them visually stunning.

1. Types of Edible Glitter

- Shimmer Dust: Provides a subtle shine.
- Metallic Dust: Creates a bold, reflective finish.
- Disco Glitter: Adds dramatic sparkle for special occasions.

2. Application Techniques
- Dry Application: Brush glitter onto confections using a food-safe brush.
- Wet Application: Mix glitter with a small amount of clear alcohol or extract and paint onto surfaces.
- Sprinkling: Dust glitter over wet icing or chocolate for a sparkling finish.

3. Tips
- Use glitter sparingly to enhance designs without overwhelming them.
- Choose FDA-approved edible glitter for safety.

Creative Applications

1. Wedding Cakes
- Use isomalt to create sugar flowers or lace appliqués.
- Airbrush gradients for ombre effects on fondant-covered cakes.

2. Holiday Desserts
- Add edible glitter to cookies or chocolates for a festive touch.
- Use spun sugar to create snow-like decorations for winter-themed desserts.

3. Centerpieces
- Craft sugar sculptures as eye-catching table decorations.
- Incorporate edible lace into dessert displays for added elegance.

Troubleshooting Advanced Techniques

1. Crystallized Isomalt
- Cause: Impurities or stirring during cooking.
- Solution: Use clean tools and avoid stirring once the isomalt has dissolved.

2. Brittle Edible Lace
- Cause: Overcooking or uneven application.
- Solution: Monitor temperature closely and spread the mixture evenly.

3. Melted Spun Sugar
- Cause: Exposure to humidity.

- Solution: Store in a dry, airtight container with desiccant packs.

Conclusion

Advanced confectionery techniques like working with isomalt, creating edible lace and spun sugar, and mastering airbrushing and edible glitter elevate your sweets into true works of art. These methods require precision, practice, and creativity, but the results are worth the effort. With the guidance provided in this chapter, you can transform your confectionery into visually stunning creations that dazzle and delight. Whether crafting showpieces for special occasions or experimenting with new techniques, let your imagination guide you in the art of advanced confectionery.

Chapter 14: Pairing Confectionery with Drinks

Pairing confectionery with drinks is an art that elevates both the sweets and the beverages, creating a symphony of flavors and textures. From delicate teas and robust coffees to sparkling wines and bold spirits, the right pairings can transform an ordinary treat into an extraordinary experience. This chapter explores the principles of pairing confectionery with tea, coffee, wine, and cocktails, provides recipes for Espresso Caramels, Champagne Truffles, and Whiskey Fudge, and offers tips for balancing flavors and intensities to achieve perfect harmony.

The Art of Pairing Confectionery with Drinks

1. Why Pair Confectionery with Drinks?

- Enhances Flavor Profiles: The right pairing can highlight complementary or contrasting flavors.

- Creates a Sensory Experience: Combining textures, aromas, and flavors enriches the overall experience.

- Adds Sophistication: Pairing sweets with drinks elevates desserts to a refined level, perfect for special occasions.

2. Principles of Pairing

- Balance: Match the intensity of the confectionery with the strength of the drink. A rich, chocolatey fudge pairs well with bold coffee, while a delicate fruit tart complements light tea.

- Contrast: Opposing flavors, like sweet and bitter or rich and acidic, create dynamic pairings.

- Complement: Pair similar flavors, such as caramel with whiskey or citrus with sparkling wine, to enhance harmony.

3. Understanding Flavor Profiles

- Sweetness: Balances bitter or acidic drinks like black coffee or dry champagne.

- Bitterness: Found in dark chocolate or coffee-infused treats, pairs well with sweet or fruity drinks.

- Acidity: In fruit-based confections, complements creamy or rich drinks like lattes.

- Richness: Found in fudges or truffles, requires bold drinks like espresso or red wine.

Pairing Sweets with Tea

Tea is a versatile drink with a wide range of flavors, from light and floral to bold and earthy. Selecting the right confectionery enhances the tea-drinking experience.

1. Popular Tea Varieties and Pairings

- Black Tea: Pairs well with rich, buttery confections like shortbread or caramel.

- Green Tea: Complements light, citrusy candies or matcha-infused treats.

- Herbal Tea: Matches fruit-based confections, such as berry gummies or orange-flavored truffles.

- Chai Tea: Its spiced profile pairs beautifully with gingerbread or cinnamon fudge.

2. Tips for Pairing with Tea

- Avoid overly sweet confections that overpower delicate teas.

- Choose complementary flavors to highlight the tea's nuances.

Pairing Sweets with Coffee

Coffee's robust and bitter profile makes it an excellent companion to a wide variety of confections.

1. Popular Coffee Varieties and Pairings

- Espresso: Pairs perfectly with dark chocolate truffles, caramels, or biscotti.

- Cappuccino: Complements creamy, light confections like vanilla fudge or macarons.

- Latte: Works well with nutty or spiced treats, such as almond brittle or cinnamon rolls.

- Cold Brew: Matches fruity confections or coffee-infused candies.

2. Tips for Pairing with Coffee

- Use sweetness to balance coffee's bitterness.

- Match the richness of the confection to the strength of the coffee.

Pairing Sweets with Wine

Wine and sweets can create a luxurious pairing when matched thoughtfully. Consider the sweetness, acidity, and flavor complexity of both the wine and the confectionery.

1. Popular Wine Types and Pairings

- Red Wine: Rich, dark chocolate or spiced confections complement bold reds like Cabernet Sauvignon.

- White Wine: Light, fruity candies pair well with crisp whites like Sauvignon Blanc.

- Rosé: Works beautifully with berry-flavored truffles or citrus gummies.

- Sparkling Wine: Champagne pairs exquisitely with delicate treats like macarons or white chocolate truffles.

2. Tips for Pairing with Wine

- Match sweetness levels: Sweet wines pair best with sweet confections, while dry wines match less sugary treats.

- Consider acidity: Fruit-based confections pair well with wines that have bright acidity.

Pairing Sweets with Cocktails

Cocktails offer bold and complex flavors that can elevate the experience of enjoying confections.

1. Popular Cocktails and Pairings

- Old Fashioned: Pairs with nutty or caramel-based confections like pralines or whiskey fudge.

- Margarita: Complements citrusy sweets like lemon bars or lime gummies.

- Espresso Martini: Enhances coffee-flavored treats like tiramisu truffles or espresso caramels.

- Pina Colada: Matches tropical candies like coconut fudge or pineapple gummies.

2. Tips for Pairing with Cocktails

- Use the cocktail's main ingredient as inspiration for the confectionery flavor.

- Balance sweetness to avoid overwhelming the palate.

Recipes

1. Espresso Caramels

Rich and chewy, these caramels have a deep coffee flavor that pairs perfectly with espresso or cappuccino.

Ingredients:

- 2 cups granulated sugar
- 1/2 cup light corn syrup
- 1/4 cup water
- 1 cup heavy cream
- 1/2 cup unsalted butter
- 2 tablespoons espresso powder
- 1 teaspoon vanilla extract

Instructions:

1. Combine sugar, corn syrup, and water in a saucepan. Heat over medium heat, stirring until sugar dissolves.

2. Add cream, butter, and espresso powder. Cook until the mixture reaches 245°F (firm ball stage).

3. Remove from heat and stir in vanilla.

4. Pour into a greased pan and let cool. Cut into squares and wrap in wax paper.

2. Champagne Truffles

These elegant truffles are infused with champagne, making them ideal for celebrations.

Ingredients:

- 8 oz white chocolate, finely chopped
- 1/4 cup heavy cream
- 2 tablespoons champagne or sparkling wine
- 1/4 cup powdered sugar (for coating)

Instructions:

1. Heat cream in a saucepan until simmering. Pour over white chocolate and stir until smooth.

2. Stir in champagne and refrigerate for 1 hour.

3. Roll teaspoon-sized portions into balls and coat with powdered sugar.

3. Whiskey Fudge

This creamy fudge has a bold whiskey flavor, perfect for pairing with an Old Fashioned or neat whiskey.

Ingredients:

- 2 cups granulated sugar
- 3/4 cup heavy cream
- 1/2 cup unsalted butter
- 1/4 cup whiskey
- 8 oz semisweet chocolate, chopped

Instructions:

1. Combine sugar, cream, and butter in a saucepan. Heat over medium heat, stirring until sugar dissolves.

2. Cook until the mixture reaches 240°F (soft ball stage).

3. Remove from heat and stir in whiskey and chocolate until smooth.

4. Pour into a greased pan and let cool. Cut into squares.

Balancing Flavors and Intensities

1. Matching Intensity

   - Pair bold confections with strong drinks, such as espresso or whiskey.

- Match light, delicate sweets with subtle drinks like green tea or champagne.

2. Enhancing Contrast

- Use sweet confections to balance bitter or acidic drinks.

- Contrast creamy treats with bubbly or crisp beverages.

3. Adding Complexity

- Incorporate complementary flavors, such as fruit in confections to mirror wine notes.

- Layer flavors in cocktails to echo the complexity of the paired candy.

Hosting a Pairing Event

1. Planning the Menu

- Select a range of confections and drinks to showcase different pairing styles.

- Include a mix of complementary and contrasting flavors.

2. Presentation Tips

- Serve confections on elegant platters with labels for each pairing.

- Offer tasting notes to guide guests through the experience.

3. Interactive Elements

- Allow guests to experiment with their own pairings.

- Provide a demonstration of candy-making techniques.

Conclusion

Pairing confectionery with drinks transforms sweets into sophisticated delights, creating memorable culinary experiences. By understanding the principles of flavor balance and intensity, you can craft perfect pairings with tea, coffee, wine, and cocktails. With recipes like Espresso Caramels, Champagne Truffles, and Whiskey Fudge, and tips for enhancing the experience, this chapter empowers you to elevate your confectionery game. Whether hosting a pairing event or enjoying a quiet treat at home, these techniques and recipes will ensure every bite and sip are in perfect harmony.

Chapter 15: Troubleshooting and Perfecting Your Craft

Confectionery is an intricate blend of science and art, requiring precision, creativity, and practice. While the rewards are sweet and satisfying, the process can sometimes be fraught with challenges. From grainy caramel to deflated marshmallows, every candy maker faces obstacles. This chapter focuses on troubleshooting common confectionery issues, fine-tuning recipes for consistency and flavor, and encouraging creativity and experimentation to take your candy-making skills to new heights.

Common Confectionery Challenges and Solutions

1. Sugar Crystallization

The Problem: Sugar crystallization occurs when sugar molecules regroup, leading to a grainy texture in candies like caramel and fudge.

Causes:

- Stirring the sugar mixture while it's boiling.

- Presence of impurities or undissolved sugar crystals.

- Lack of stabilizing agents like corn syrup.

Solutions:

1. Preventative Measures:

- Use a clean, heavy-bottomed saucepan.

- Brush down the sides of the pan with a damp pastry brush to dissolve stray sugar crystals.

- Avoid stirring the mixture once it begins to boil.

2. Incorporate Stabilizers:

- Add corn syrup, honey, or lemon juice to disrupt sugar crystal formation.

3. Fixing Crystallized Mixtures:

- Reheat the mixture with a few tablespoons of water and dissolve the sugar again.

2. Grainy Fudge

The Problem: Fudge with a coarse, grainy texture instead of a smooth, creamy consistency.

Causes:

- Undercooking or overcooking the sugar syrup.

- Stirring too early during the cooling process.

Solutions:

1. Cook the sugar syrup to the correct temperature (235–240°F, soft ball stage) using a candy thermometer.

2. Allow the mixture to cool undisturbed to 110°F before beating.

3. Beat until the fudge loses its gloss and thickens but avoid overmixing.

3. Sticky or Runny Caramel

The Problem: Caramel is too soft, sticky, or doesn't set properly.

Causes:

- Undercooking the caramel (not reaching the proper temperature).

- Excess liquid in the recipe.

Solutions:

1. Use a thermometer to ensure the caramel reaches 245–250°F for chewy caramel or 300°F for firm caramel.

2. Reduce the liquid in the recipe slightly or increase the cooking time.

4. Burnt Sugar

The Problem: Sugar burns easily during caramelization, leading to a bitter taste.

Causes:

- Cooking sugar at too high a heat.

- Leaving sugar unattended while cooking.

Solutions:

1. Cook sugar over medium heat for better control.

2. Stir gently until sugar dissolves, then stop stirring to prevent uneven caramelization.

3. Keep a close eye on the sugar's color—it should be golden amber, not dark brown.

5. Sticky or Deflated Marshmallows

The Problem: Marshmallows turn out sticky or fail to hold their shape.

Causes:

- Inadequate whipping time.

- Excess humidity during the setting process.

Solutions:

1. Whip the marshmallow mixture until thick and fluffy (about 10 minutes).

2. Coat the marshmallows generously with a mixture of powdered sugar and cornstarch.

3. Allow marshmallows to set in a cool, dry place.

6. Brittles That Don't Crack

The Problem: Brittle is soft and chewy instead of crisp and snappable.

Causes:

- Not cooking the sugar syrup to the hard crack stage (300°F).

- Excess moisture in the mixture.

Solutions:

1. Ensure the sugar syrup reaches 300°F before adding nuts or spreading the mixture.

2. Work quickly to spread the brittle before it cools.

Fine-Tuning Recipes for Consistency and Flavor

1. Balancing Sweetness

Too much sweetness can overwhelm flavors in confectionery. Balance sweetness by:

- Adding a pinch of salt to enhance complexity.

- Incorporating acidic ingredients like citrus or tart berries to cut through sweetness.

- Using bittersweet chocolate or coffee for depth.

2. Enhancing Flavor

Maximize flavor by:

- Toasting nuts before adding them to brittles, fudges, or nougat for a deeper flavor.

- Infusing creams or syrups with spices, herbs, or citrus zest for added complexity.

- Experimenting with extracts, like almond, vanilla, or peppermint, for tailored results.

3. Adjusting Texture

- For Creaminess: Use more butter, cream, or milk in recipes like fudge or caramels.

- For Crunch: Add mix-ins like nuts, seeds, or crispy rice.

- For Chewiness: Incorporate additional gelatin or corn syrup in recipes like gummies.

4. Perfecting Appearance

- Use molds for uniform shapes and designs.

- Dip confections in tempered chocolate for a glossy finish.

- Decorate with edible glitter, gold leaf, or colored sprinkles to enhance visual appeal.

Encouraging Creativity in Candy-Making

1. Experiment with Flavors

Don't be afraid to go beyond traditional flavors. Try:

- Exotic spices like cardamom, saffron, or star anise.

- Floral notes like lavender, rosewater, or orange blossom.

- Savory additions like smoked salt, chili powder, or bacon bits.

2. Play with Colors

- Use gel-based food coloring for vibrant hues in marshmallows, lollipops, or gummies.

- Experiment with natural dyes, like beet juice (red), turmeric (yellow), or matcha powder (green).

3. Try New Techniques

Advanced techniques like sugar pulling, airbrushing, or creating edible lace can push your skills further. Take time to:

- Practice shaping sugar into flowers, ribbons, or abstract designs.

- Learn to use an airbrush for ombre effects on candies.

4. Innovate with Mix-Ins
- Add dried fruits, seeds, or chopped cookies for texture and flavor.
- Swirl caramel or fruit jam into fudge for a marbled effect.

Learning from Mistakes

Mistakes are inevitable but valuable learning experiences. Keep a candy-making journal to:

1. Record recipes and notes on what worked or didn't.
2. Track changes in ingredient proportions or cooking times.
3. Develop new ideas based on past experiments.

Building Confidence and Mastery

1. Start Simple

Begin with basic recipes like fudge or brittle, then progress to advanced techniques like marshmallow-making or sugar art.

2. Practice Consistency

Repeat recipes multiple times to perfect techniques and timing.

3. Gather Feedback

Share your creations with friends and family to gain constructive feedback.

Essential Tools for Perfecting Your Craft

1. Candy Thermometer: For precise temperature control.
2. Silicone Mats: Non-stick surfaces ideal for sugar work.
3. Heat-Resistant Spatulas: Essential for mixing hot sugar or chocolate.
4. Molds and Cutters: For shaping and customizing confections.

Celebrating Your Confectionery Journey

Candy-making is as much about the process as the final product. Celebrate your journey by:
- Documenting your creations with photographs or a blog.
- Participating in local fairs or competitions.
- Sharing your knowledge through classes or workshops.

Conclusion

Mastering confectionery is a rewarding journey of skill, creativity, and experimentation. By understanding common challenges and learning how to overcome them, fine-tuning recipes for flavor and texture, and embracing the spirit of innovation, you can take your candy-making to professional levels. Every mistake is a step toward mastery, and every creation is a testament to your dedication. Let this chapter inspire you to perfect your craft and explore the limitless possibilities of confectionery.

Conclusion: Celebrating the Art of Confectionery

Confectionery is more than the act of making sweet treats; it's a timeless craft that brings joy, creativity, and a touch of magic to our lives. From the first steps of mastering sugar's science to the advanced techniques of crafting edible art, candy-making is a journey filled with discovery and delight. It bridges generations, evokes nostalgia, and celebrates life's sweetest moments. As we conclude this exploration into the world of confectionery, let us celebrate the artistry, encourage continued exploration and creativity, and offer resources to inspire your ongoing journey.

The Timeless Craft of Confectionery

1. A Legacy of Sweetness

Confectionery has been a part of human culture for centuries, evolving from simple honey-coated nuts in ancient times to the intricate sugar sculptures of the Renaissance. Each sweet tells a story, reflecting the traditions, flavors, and innovations of its time and place.

2. Universal Appeal

Sweets transcend language and cultural barriers, making confectionery a universal language of joy. Whether it's a caramel enjoyed during a quiet moment or a celebratory cake shared among friends, confectionery unites people in happiness.

3. A Blend of Science and Art

Candy-making requires precision, patience, and a deep understanding of ingredients, yet it also offers endless opportunities for creativity and personal expression. It's a craft that combines technical mastery with artistic imagination.

Encouragement to Explore and Create

1. Embrace Experimentation

Confectionery is as much about exploration as it is about technique. Don't be afraid to:

- Experiment with bold flavors, like combining unexpected ingredients such as chili and chocolate.

- Try new techniques, whether it's pulling sugar for ribbons or mastering airbrushing.

- Adapt traditional recipes to reflect your unique taste and style.

2. Share the Joy

One of the most rewarding aspects of candy-making is sharing your creations with others. Handmade confections are a tangible expression of care and thoughtfulness, making them perfect for:

- Celebrating special occasions like birthdays, weddings, and holidays.

- Creating cherished traditions, such as making fudge for family gatherings or gifting marshmallows during the winter season.

3. Turn Failures into Learning Opportunities

Every candy-maker has faced challenges, from burnt sugar to collapsed marshmallows. These moments are not failures but steps toward mastery. Document your experiences, learn from your mistakes, and celebrate your progress.

Inspiring Creativity in Confectionery

1. Think Beyond the Recipe

While recipes provide a foundation, the magic happens when you make them your own. Add your personality to your creations through:

- Unique flavor combinations (e.g., lavender and lemon, or cardamom and pistachio).

- Creative shapes and designs that match themes or occasions.

- Personalized packaging that reflects your style.

2. Incorporate Seasonal and Local Ingredients

Using seasonal fruits, herbs, and spices not only enhances flavor but also grounds your confections in a sense of time and place. Think of:

- Citrus-flavored gummies in summer.

- Spiced caramel for autumn.

- Berry truffles in spring.

- Peppermint bark in winter.

3. Explore Global Inspirations

The world of confectionery is vast, with countless traditions to draw from. Try making:

- Japanese mochi for its chewy texture and subtle sweetness.

- Middle Eastern halva for its nutty, crumbly richness.

- French nougat for its elegance and airiness.

Sharing Sweet Treats with Loved Ones

1. The Joy of Gifting

Homemade candy is one of the most heartfelt gifts. From beautifully wrapped truffles to jars of colorful lollipops, sweets convey love and care. Personalize your gifts with:

- Handwritten recipe cards.

- Custom labels or packaging.

- Thoughtful pairings, like chocolate-covered pretzels alongside a favorite tea blend.

2. Hosting Confectionery-Themed Gatherings

Candy-making can be a social activity that brings people together. Organize events such as:

- Candy-Making Parties: Let guests make their own candies, from caramels to marshmallows.

- Tasting Evenings: Pair homemade confections with wines, teas, or coffees.

- Workshops for Kids: Teach children the basics of confectionery with simple and fun projects like candy necklaces or marshmallows.

Resources for Further Learning and Inspiration

1. Books and Guides

Expand your knowledge with books that cover specific areas of confectionery:

- "On Food and Cooking" by Harold McGee: A deep dive into the science behind food, including candy-making.

- "The Art of French Pastry" by Jacquy Pfeiffer: A detailed guide to elegant pastries and confections.

- "Chocolates and Confections" by Peter Greweling: A comprehensive resource for mastering chocolate work.

2. Online Tutorials and Communities

The internet offers countless resources for candy-makers of all levels:

- YouTube Channels: Search for tutorials on advanced techniques like sugar pulling or tempering chocolate.

- Social Media Groups: Join confectionery-focused communities to share ideas, ask questions, and gain inspiration.

- Blogs and Websites: Explore recipe blogs that specialize in creative and innovative sweets.

3. Classes and Workshops

Attending a class or workshop can provide hands-on experience and direct guidance:

- Local culinary schools often offer short courses on confectionery.

- Specialty confectionery shops may host workshops or demonstrations.

- Online platforms like MasterClass or Skillshare feature professional candy-makers.

4. Tools and Equipment

Invest in quality tools to refine your craft:

- Candy thermometers for precision.

- Airbrushes and molds for decoration.

- High-quality ingredients like couverture chocolate and pure vanilla extract to elevate flavor.

Final Thoughts

Confectionery is a craft that combines tradition, science, and art to create moments of joy and connection. Whether you're a beginner making your first batch of fudge or an experienced candy-maker experimenting with sugar art, the journey is as rewarding as the destination. Celebrate your successes, learn from your challenges, and always find delight in the process.

Let your creativity flourish, share your sweet creations with loved ones, and continue to explore the endless possibilities of confectionery. With each treat you make, you're not only crafting something delicious—you're creating memories, traditions, and a legacy of sweetness. Here's to the art of confectionery, a timeless craft that brings joy to life's simplest and grandest moments.

"The only thing sweeter than candy is the happiness it brings. Keep creating, keep sharing, and keep celebrating the art of confectionery."

Don't miss out!

Visit the website below and you can sign up to receive emails whenever Olivia Bennett publishes a new book. There's no charge and no obligation.

https://books2read.com/r/B-A-QLEKD-VSPAG

BOOKS2READ

Connecting independent readers to independent writers.

About the Author

Olivia Bennett is a celebrated food writer and chef with expertise spanning multiple culinary disciplines. With a passion for making home cooking accessible, she specializes in guiding readers through everything from hearty casseroles to delicate pastries. Her work is known for its clear instructions, practical tips, and deep understanding of both traditional and modern cooking techniques.